D1399456

never shake
hands with
a war criminal

barry crimmins

never shake hands with a war criminal

SEVEN STORIES PRESS

New York • London • Toronto • Melbourne

Dedicated to Howard Zinn. Many people make history; few people change it.

Page 140 epigraph from "Your Flag Decal (Won't Get You into Heaven Anymore)" © 1971 by John Prine. Used by permission of Ohboy Records, Nashville.

Seven Stories Press
140 Watts Street
New York, NY 10013
www.sevenstories.com

IN THE UNITED STATES
Consortium Book Sales and Distibution, 1045 Westgate Drive, St. Paul, MN 55114

IN CANADA
Publishers Group Canada, 250A Carlton Street, Toronto, Ontario M5A 2L1

IN THE UK
Turnaround Publisher Services Ltd., Unit 3, Olympia Trading Estate, Coburg Road, Wood Green, London N22 6TZ

IN AUSTRALIA
Palgrave Macmillan, 627 Chapel Street, South Yarra VIC 3141

College professors may order examination copies of Seven Stories Press titles for a free six-month trial period. To order, visit www.sevenstories.com/textbook/ or fax on school letterhead to 212.226.1411.

LIBRARY OF CONGRESS CATALOGING-IN-PUBLICATION DATA
Crimmins, Barry.
Never shake hands with a war criminal / Barry Crimmins.—A Seven Stories Press 1st ed.
   p. cm.
ISBN 1-58322-660-5 (hardcover)
1. American wit and humor. 2. Crimmins, Barry. 3. Humorists—United States—Biography. 4. Radio broadcasters—United States—Biography. I. Title.
PN6165.C75 2004
791.4402'8'092—dc22   2004017289

9 8 7 6 5 4 3 2 1

Book design by India Amos
Printed in Canada

contents

never shake
hands with
a war criminal

An angry audience member asked, "If you don't love this country, why don't you get out?"

I replied, "Because I don't want to be victimized by its foreign policy."

Even in death, Nixon is like herpes—each time you think he's gone, he flares up again.

Too many Americans think wrestling is real and war is fake.

I'm a proponent of gun control. For those of you in the National Rifle Association, "proponent" means I'm *in favor* of gun control.

There's a nickel's worth of difference between Democrats and Republicans. If you put a nickel on the table, a Democrat will steal it from you . . . and a Republican will kill you for it.

one

Syracuse Has a Foot,
Maybe Twelve Inches of Snow

Mark Twain promised that there'd be no weather in his novel *The American Claimant*. In a hilarious disclaimer he made a good point about how literature is rife with needless descriptions of meteorological circumstances. Anyone who has read the book knows that Mr. Clemens shattered his pledge and used weather as the central issue at the story's conclusion.

Old Sam can't be blamed. The elements are hard to avoid, particularly in my hometown of Skaneateles, New York, located on the northern tip of the lake of the same name. It buckles under the same snowbelt that Syracuse has immortalized. Just to the north, Lake Ontario runs almost perfectly east-west on the border with Canada, ideally situated to create lake-effect snow. The other Great Lakes lie at more of an angle. That's why the least of the Greats creates the most consistently tyrannical winters: Its paralleling of the northern boundary provides a short commute for icy gales that mix with lake moisture to become more snow than most of you will ever see. And this is *before* Christmas.

It isn't until the New Year that winter truly begins to weed out the weak. Alberta Clippers and lake-effect blizzards are sensational, but it's the relentlessness of the most miserable of seasons that breaks people. Marriages dissolve, friendships collapse, businesses fail. Many just sit in their homes and drink until it becomes possible to open the door again. In years when the snowfall reaches fifteen feet, cirrhosis may set in before that happens.

As if the lake-effects dumpings weren't sufficient, Skaneateles is close enough to the Atlantic Ocean to catch the brunt of many nor'easters. Most years there will be a terrible week when two lake-provoked blizzards bracket a nor'easter. Some years it will snow every day for several weeks. Most years the snow starts early and leaves late. I've seen serious snow on Memorial Day weekend and on several Halloweens, where the only believable costume was that of the Michelin Man. In January even mercury heads south to huddle in the little ball at the bottom of the thermometer. At this point winter becomes sarcastic. When it warms up, it snows. Temperatures upward of twenty degrees feel like a balmy spring day.

Worse than the arctic temps and mountains of precipitation is the pathological lack of sunshine. Those allergic to sunlight are sent to live in Central New York, a place where photo-toxicity will keep an individual housebound for only a few weeks a year. One-hundred plus inches of annual snowfall is tough, but it's the dreariness that really gets to you. The c n y skies turn battleship gray in late October and rarely appear otherwise until the middle of April.

Cynicism peaks in February, when it feels as if it has been winter since you were a small child. People begin to fearfully discuss 1816, the year "summer never came." It actually did come, but sporadic frosts that were the long-term result of the 1815 eruption of the Tambora volcano, east of Java but well west of Rochester, ruined crops throughout the northeast. Atmospheric ash reduced sunlight, and it never really warmed up that year. Because there is a precedent, a latter-day endless winter becomes one of the few possibilities that seem believable during January here in the Finger Lakes. Spending so much time cooped up and bummed out leads one down the contrarian path. This is understandable, since it's one of the few passages that do not require shoveling three times a day. So people from Central New York spend a lot of time carefully examining things—for flaws. When I was growing up, the three Syracuse TV stations offered a very narrow amount of programming. We saw most of it again and again. We always spotted the newscaster with the toupee, the high-tension wires in tales of the Old West, and the sportscasters who said ridiculous things like, "Syracuse has a foot, maybe *twelve inches* to go for a first down."

These things were absurd, and when we focused on them and improvised around them, we laughed. While laughing, we forgot that there were only three and a half months until spring. And that if we could see the sun, it would still set at about 3:00 PM. The local accent, with its defeated and flattened tone, is also weather related. It contributes mightily to the general malaise. It's hard to say, "a hundred and ninety-three inches of snow" crisply. The phrase must be dragged out, just like winter. A hunnnerdaaannd-nyyyyndeeeetreee innnnchaaazzz aaaaa snoooohhhh. Wait, now it's a hunnnerdaaanndnyyyyndeeeefourrrr innnnchaaazzz aaaaa snoooohhhh.

Teachers at Skaneateles Central School fought the elements just to reach classrooms full of third graders capable of scoffing, "Yeah, sure" with sardonic eloquence. SCS students can take a word like "probably" and turn it into a weapon of mass farcification. "Oh yeah, we're praaaahblee gonna play owtside taaaday." I was one of those third graders. And so weather has made me what I am today—which is to say, skeptical. And just a tad sarcastic.

Dateline December, 2001

Can it really be a year since we didn't elect George W. Bush president? Time sure flies when you're going straight to hell.

Laura Bush announced that she would use her position as First Lady to promote abstinence. No one wondered why.

February's highlight came when the teaching of evolution was restored in Kansas. Kansans celebrated by walking upright, taking shelter from storms, and communicating through a series of simple grunts. If this keeps up, their congressional delegation is in big trouble.

In March, Bush announced that taxes on the rich would be replaced with an honor system under which the elite would be expected to increase their commitment to private, faith-based bribery and slush funds by some 50 percent.

The aircraft carrier USS *Ronald Reagan* was christened and immediately manned by scab air-traffic controllers. The vessel is actually larger than Grenada, the site of Reagan's greatest military victory.

A March earthquake heavily damaged Starbucks' Seattle headquarters. Within days the coffee giant bounced back and replaced it with sixty new headquarters at various places around the city.

The administration failed to explain adequately the "Baptists under fire" incident in Peru, where a Baptist missionary's plane was shot down under the aegis of narcotics interdiction. Apparently the War on Drugs targeted-substance list had been expanded to include "opiate of the masses."

First the Bush administration literally takes office and then *The Producers* sweeps the Tonys. The year 2001 will always be remembered for joke revivals featuring fascists.

Jenna Bush was busted in June for underage drinking. Considering who her father is, it's a miracle the poor kid isn't walking around with a morphine drip in her elbow.

Unlike most Americans in their first year on a new job, W. took an extended paid holiday in August. It's a good thing he got rested up, rather than exhausting himself with concerns like airport safety and domestic security.

American Tragedy As Cool Photo Op

We've all heard about the Republican National Committee's direct-mail piece offering donors three photographs of court-appointed President Bush, including one of him on Air Force One on September 11 as he hightailed it out of harm's way while his nation was under attack.

Kind of makes you pine for the good old days, when all that might have turned up in your mailbox was anthrax or a bomb, doesn't it?

The Air Force One shot *is* a rare photo. In the background, actual Bush spin doctors are concocting the very lies they told us on September 12 to explain away why Bush went Barney Fife on September 11. According to the GOP letter, the three pictures depict:

- ". . . the gritty determination of our new president at his inauguration" (as he bravely appears in public in shoes he tied himself).

- ". . . a telephone call from Air Force One to Vice President Cheney on the afternoon of Sept. 11, 2001." (*But I'm a-scared to come home, Unka Dick*).

- ". . . and President Bush's historic State of the Union speech before a joint session of Congress that united a nation and a world" (in disgust over his inane "axis of evil" allegations).

In light of the shocking news that George W. Bush actually knew something (or anything), the Republican National
Committee should withdraw the offer of photos of Bush on the
Day He Should Have Seen Coming and add some other shots
as premiums:

- Tax Haven, Connecticut, 1946: Little George is born with a
  silver spoon in . . . his nose.

- Anywhere but Texas, 1972: Over hill, over dale, Dubster hits
  the dusty trail as he goes AWOL from the National Guard.

- Port Pickle, Maine, 1976: W stands for "weave," as far as the
  officer administering this field sobriety test is concerned.

- Midscam, Texas, 1978: The only strikes made by Jr. Oilman
  Bush are at the bank accounts of investors in one failed scheme
  after another.

- Texican Border, 1983: W has yet to find God but does meet
  up with CIA operative and close family friend Crankisco de
  Muerto, who provides Jr. with all the "inspiration" he needs
  to stay ever vigilant in case the Sandinistas make a move.

- Arlington Depths, Texas, 1992: George brandishes a genuine
  Louisville Slugger as he drives residents from their homes to
  make way for the taxpayer-funded ballpark in Arlington, which
  helped turn his $600,000 investment in the Texas Rangers base-
  ball team into over fifteen million publicly subsidized dollars
  when he sold his interest in the franchise a few years later.

- Lynchland County, Texas, 1998: On his trip from the Death
  House to the White House, Texas governor Bush stops to
  apologize to close pal "Kenny Boy" Lay for not switching the

Lone Star State's method of execution from lethal injection to the electric chair, thereby depriving Enron of a chance to profiteer on the statewide brownouts that surely would have followed.

• Republican Nationalist Convention 2000: the bowels of hell actually open to reveal a chortling Satan as Bush promises to return ethics to Washington. In the past this had only happened when W claimed to be either an environmentalist or a compassionate conservative.

• Presidential suite Casa de Polloguano, Polloguano, Texas, November 7, 2000: Jr. asks his brother, "Paper or plastic?" Jeb patiently explains that "Florida is in the bag" is just a figure of speech.

But then, maybe those photos would be better suited for *Democratic* fundraising.

Not that the photos already chosen couldn't serve Dem purposes as well. Could the R's have selected a worse moment to commemorate than the September 11 photo of Bush boogying to Nebraska? In it, he's pictured dutifully phoning chief handler Dick Cheney while the nation, for which he was supposedly responsible, was under attack. The picture captures Bush's cowardice and subservience—which is to say, his essence. Democrats generally have to speak at an American Israel Public Affairs Committee event to appear even a fraction as compromised.

It's not as if the Republicans were forced into hawking the Bush photos out of economic necessity. On May 14 the party raised a cool $30 million at a corporate fundraiser. Wasn't that act of political prostitution enough? Did they really have to stoop so low as to turn September 11 into a special collector's item? Of course they did; they're Republicans, and to them sleaze equals virtue.

So on the very day that news of the Bush photo offer hit the wires, the R's held a black-tie gala to celebrate their sliminess. The most emotional part of the evening came when Bush asked for a moment of silence in honor of all the Enron and Arthur Andersen officials who couldn't be there to gorge themselves as they had at so many earlier events. A spotlight shone on two empty black valises during the hushed salute.

Even without the Kenny Boy contingent there were still plenty of black-tied bagmen to exert undue influence on an administration that always gets list price for its services. The $100,000–to–$250,000 donors at the May 14 Glutton Cotillion, no doubt already in possession of framed and autographed copies of the September 11 photo of Bush hotfooting it to the game room in Nebraska, included: American International Group, Chevron, the El Paso Corporation, Microsoft, Philip Morris, American Auto Parts, NVR Inc., Union Pacific, the American Hospital Association, AT&T, Cigna, Dominion, FirstEnergy, Lockheed Martin, and Schering-Plough.

So the next time you get mistreated, fleeced, sickened, or downsized by an insurance company, software giant, oil gargantuan, transportation concern, big tobacco, health-care depriver, communications monolith, real-estate Goliath, heartless bank, energy speculator, weapons contractor, or pharmaceutical peddler, close your eyes and visualize our court-appointed president using Air Force One to flee like a cockroach skittering away from a suddenly illuminated room. It's all you'll have. When this crew gets done ripping you off, you certainly won't be able to afford an official RNC print.

2001 Cont'd

On September 11, the whole world changed—except for large portions of Europe, Asia, and Africa, several island nations, and those parts of the world where terrorism, whether state-sponsored or rogue, was already part of everyday life. Okay, on September 11 life in the United States began to resemble, just slightly, life elsewhere.

The prez was addressing elementary-school children in Florida when the attacks occurred; for some reason he kept addressing them despite the calamitous events. (Somehow it's always Florida.) He then headed to Louisiana and finally into a game room in Omaha.

I might have given Bush a pass on going Barney Fife that morning except for a few things. During a time when even Rudolph Giuliani rose above venal political considerations (albeit briefly), the Bush administration's apparent top priority was to propagate alibis about why the president headed for the Grain Belt while the Northeast Corridor burned. This included telling us about a call to the Secret Service stating that the president was in imminent danger. Problem is, no such call was received. Bush was supposed to be a hard-ass Texas Republican naturally inclined to fly to DC, climb to the roof of the White House, and wave pearl-handled revolvers, yelling, "Try me, motherfuckers!" Instead, the Incredible President Limpet headed for a bunker in the Central Time Zone.

On September 12, while uncounted victims lay trapped under piles of rubble, several administration officials spent the morning telling us about the mythical phone threat, along with other prevarications that must have taken much of September 11 to prepare.

Within days, even most skeptics were convinced that Osama bin Laden was behind the terrorist attacks. The United States vowed to bring him to justice. All searches should include probes into the curdled milk of human kindness—a sure sign he's nearby. If that doesn't work, go to Jerry Falwell and take a slight right. If you get to Ann Coulter, you've gone too far.

Americans cautiously returned to airports to face many inconveniences. The new rule of thumb for airline passengers is to allow yourself as much time as it would take to walk to your destination.

At around the same time someone decided that all motor vehicles should enter a General-Patton-staff-car look-alike contest. The fiercest competition was among sport-utility vehicles. Americans, involved in a war that's in no small part related to dependence on Middle Eastern oil, managed to make obscenely fuel-inefficient suvs that much worse with the addition of red, white, and blue wind resistance.

three

The Beginning of the Endless

O n February 22, 2001, Karen Crist, my love interest, and noted barrister, Lloyd the Dog, and I arrived at the extremely rural home we rented in Troupsburg, New York, a few hours southwest of Skaneateles, while beginning the search for a more permanent domicile. It was a shock to return upstate and find town after town in economic shambles. An exodus of jobs that had begun during my childhood had continued apace and devastated the region. These days, if you're lucky, you'll find work at a prison or a Wal-Mart. I have a hard time distinguishing one from the other, although I know the prisoners get the better health plan.

My homecoming took place just a few weeks after George W. Bush quite literally took office. When we got here, there was no snow on the ground in the rustic community on the Pennsylvania border at either the beginning or end of the Endless Mountains, depending on your perspective. It didn't snow on February 23, 2001, either. Then it snowed every day until early April. Until then I hadn't realized that "Endless" referred to snow.

The following winter of 2001–2002 was mercifully mild. Jack Frost must have been nursing a hangover from all the nips he had taken the previous spring. If he made any appearances at all, I can't remember them. Good thing—I couldn't have handled the madness of 9/11 and America's "become what we resist" response during a traditional upstate winter.

In 2002–2003 Old Man Winter returned from sabbatical with renewed ferocity. I am surviving its onslaught as I type. It's been colder than Nancy Reagan's heart and longer than Ronald Reagan's presidency. It snowed during the World Series. We haven't had one unseasonably warm day since last summer. I've been cooped up and cranky for months. My snowshoes need resoling. Of course Skaneateles has been worse. That town has had about two more feet of snow than us. But then, there were a couple of warm spells up there.

Nowadays cabin fever can be minimized by distractions unavailable during my childhood. The internet and a satellite dish bring the latest news and entertainment to my home. If I want a book, I click a few buttons and the UPS driver is here with it a few days later. I stoke the woodstove and then sit in front of the Mac or television and pick out the flaws in a much wider array of contemporary life than could be found on the Syracuse TV stations of the 1960s. My initial response to such provocation remains consistent with that of my childhood. I watch a politician give a speech and I scoff, "Yeah, sure." I read a mainstream pundit who tells me the speech was great, and I sneer, "Probably."

These are pretty awful times—by either political or meteorological measures. When I reached forty, cold weather began bothering me; it was as if my lining suddenly wore out. Before that I rarely enlisted more than a tweed sports coat to keep icy gusts at bay. One day, while shivering my way through a protest in front of a federal building in Boston, I had an epiphany: *I had been freezing my ass off for years.* I decided to do something about it. And so, with the judicious application of warm coats, hats, gloves, and boots, I was able to once again play winter to a tie. But as I neared fifty, the relentless frigidity seems capable of busting any bunker I shiver within. It has been at least minus ten degrees several times, and there have been weeks when, save for an hour or two on a few afternoons, we have not seen double digits on the sane side of zero. Going outside is akin to taking a Polaroid MRI—in just a few seconds you can tell exactly what is wrong with you. *Oh gee, I guess I do need knee-replacement surgery.*

I don't really mind being outside, especially with Lloyd, a chocolate brown lab-shepherd mix and genuine charmer. Every day is a week to a dog, and Karen and I try to make sure his weeks are wonderful. Our winter forays onto the upstate face are awful but nice. The season has always been cosmetically underrated. Once we get moving, the beauty of the crystallized appendages of a flash-frozen willow tree, the perfect symmetry of a stand of pines iced with thick dollops of snow, or the hushed splendor of a forest trail that has become a pristine white tunnel of solitude make me forget the world's troubles even as they continue arriving back at my desk at the speed of light.

This is the perfect metaphorical winter. Like the Bush administration, it is merciless and seemingly perpetual. Something worse always seems imminent. This infernal weather torments me from a place equidistant from the beginning and (please!) end of the George W. Bush's four stolen years. Like the frosted trees and hushed trails, some political beauty has emerged in these ugly times. The Internet is full of virtual freedom fighters who have not forgotten the electoral hijacking that took place in 2000. These people respond with wit and reason to each new move by a White House that has done nothing but work toward making its stolen powers boundless. Most recently these electronic activists have played an essential role in turning out massive numbers at peace marches in opposition to an administration that has created a political wind-chill factor that is meant to encase all opposing views beneath the permafrost. But we peace activists are a hardy sort and have bundled up and huddled together in a valiant effort to protect our nation's soul from frostbite. We keep faith and know that winter can't last forever. The crops did return in 1817. But still, it is a wearisome time for even the staunchest among us.

The work this winter has been for peace. The cause is desperate.

Dateline 2002

"I cannot think of a time when business overall has been held in less repute."

—Henry M. Paulson Jr., CEO of Goldman Sachs

"We're going to run the country like a corporation."
—George W. Bush, on the 2000 presidential campaign trail

The year 2002 was like a fairy tale—the *middle* of a fairy tale, when despair grows exponentially with each turn of the page.

2002: The Fairy Tale was authored by the Family Grim, a/k/a the Bushes. They got plenty of ghostwriting help from an assemblage of spooks, zealots, felons, corporate cronies, merchants of death, environmental assassins, bigots, and *retro*-retread right-wingers who rose from political caskets to reassert world views that were arcane back when Strom Thurmond was still fighting for the Confederate Army.

Enron set the platinum standard for scum. It was the business model for much of what was revealed throughout the rest of the year. Shortsighted, cold-hearted, and with a front office replete with more felons than you could fit into a crack house on a Friday night, this Ponzi scheme of a conglomerate had one business goal—to rob everyone.

Connecticut senator Joe Lieberman's former chief of staff was a lobbyist for Enron. Lieberman also received campaign and PAC contributions from the corporation that he later gently poked and prodded at some Capitol Hill hearings. Responding to calls for him to recuse himself from the Enron investigation, the indignant Lieberman sputtered, "To say Enron owns me is absurd. Anyone who knows me knows that I am first, last, and always a pawn of the *insurance* industry!"

Bush's State of the Union address included his infamous designation of Iraq, Iran, and North Korea as an "axis of evil." Iran and Iraq are blood enemies, and North Korea is far removed from both nations, being located just slightly north of South Korea. The war on this particular axis proved to be a success. There wasn't a single summit between the leaders of the three nations throughout the rest of the year.

In March, Vice President Dick Cheney was penciled in to head up the shadow government, although some questioned the move, since he himself doesn't cast one. Cheney spent much of the month on a twelve-nation war-keeping mission. The tour was fairly uneventful, except for one speech during which he chipped a fang on a microphone.

four

Time Bombed

For several weeks in the summer of 2002 I was able to put aside my outrage with the president and all the fat cats who now use 1600 Pennsylvania Avenue as their personal litter box. I had more immediate problems than the dissolution of civil liberties at home; the greed of corporations that have stolen so much that they can no longer afford employees, much less pension plans; or the poor people who will suffer as the U.S. military, in its role as twenty-first-century corporate Hessians, stomps all over the Middle East.

An emergency demanded all my physical and spiritual resources. Chris Bracken, one of the finest people I have ever known, was diagnosed with "aggressive, inoperable" liver cancer on July 5. The doctors gave him just three weeks to live.

Chris was the first friend I made after I moved to Boston in 1979. We became closer with each succeeding year, in large part because he was more laughs than a documentary about J. Edgar Hoover's private life and more reliable than any information gathered by Hoover's agency. He was the kind of there-when-needed guy who didn't have a best friend—because he had several.

In 2001 Chris had been diagnosed with colon cancer. In April 2002, after nearly a year of treatments and surgeries, he was pronounced cancer-free. But then, in July, we learned the disease never really left and probably wouldn't until it took Chris Bracken with it.

The winter was mild, but it didn't matter, Chris was generally on medication that made it unsafe for him to venture into the sun.

So he was a bit stir crazy. He staved off gloom by watching lots of his favorite show, *The Simpsons*. I took to viewing it several times a day, just to tell him which episodes had arrived via satellite dish at my extremely rural home in western New York State. At a time when we needed to take our mind off of things, the Simpsons proved ideal. Even after repeated watching, the shows revealed new, great new jokes. The less subtle ones weren't so bad either. We laughed for a month after one Springfield townsperson said to a milling crowd that they shouldn't discuss s-e-x in front of the c-h-i-l-d-r-e-n, to which Krusty the Clown responded, "Sex Cauldron? I thought they closed that place."

We spent hours just trying to figure out what the hell you'd do at a Sex Cauldron. Or in one.

When Chris was diagnosed with liver cancer, I tracked down an old friend for the first time in years. Boston native Dana Gould, a wonderfully inventive standup comic, had been working for *The Simpsons* for several years. I called him at home after a Fourth of July getaway and told him about Chris and how much he loved the Simpsons. Gould didn't even make me ask for anything, he just said, "Give me his address and I'll get something out to him."

Two days later a beautiful cell, featuring all of the Simpsons characters arrived via overnight shipping, signed by the cast as well as by Matt Groening, the show's creator. The Simpson clan was gathered at the kitchen table and several lesser characters were scattered about the rest of the scene. At a time I could do nothing for Chris, Dana did. Bracken beamed for the next couple of days, and for the rest of his life a mere glance at the artwork would bring a smile to his gaunt face.

Chris's final weeks were similar to those of many doomed people—desperately horrible and shockingly unavoidable, yet profoundly redemptive. People who knew Chris pulled together and gave all they could and then some in an attempt to save him. That included his oncologist, who'd gotten to know Chris over the past year and who wept when he had given him the liver-cancer diagnosis, and dozens of friends beating the bushes and the Internet for miracle cures (herbal and otherwise) and special comforts (late-stage-cancer patients need really super soft blankets, and so on). When it was clear that no miracle was forthcoming, they did all they could to send him off in a snug cocoon of love.

He returned the love with special words and gestures for all of us. What he did for me was let me in and let me help. He knew I couldn't sit idly by at such a moment.

He put me in charge of several people who picked up where he'd left off on a house he'd begun to construct on a Vermont mountainside. I arrived to find our dear friend Marco Romagnoli already in town, giving up a week of primo carpentry work on Cape Cod to help get Chris's project in order. Just as Marco was about to leave, my pal Kevin Mackey arrived from Detroit to help out, and he didn't even know Chris. Once he met him, Mackey stayed and toiled day and night so that the place would take shape for Chris to see before he died. Also coming up from Boston at every opportunity was Robin Hordon, a dear friend I'd made when he had just been fired as an air-traffic controller by Ronald Reagan. Hordon and Mackey put a tin roof on the entire building in two days, fighting high winds and thunderstorms each treacherous step of the way. Chris had planned to move into the completed structure with his fiancée, Amy LeBaron, and her daughter, Hali. That dream was never realized, but by the time Chris passed, we'd made the building solid and secure, sealed from the elements with sound carpentry. Dozens of others—especially Chris's family—donated time, effort, money, and materials to the cause. Amy somehow managed to come up each day and add major improvements to the landscaping of the grounds. She also regularly fattened us with some of the most scrumptious baked goods you've ever tasted.

:::

I split my time between the house and Amy's apartment, where she had bravely brought Chris home to die. As I drove back and forth on a pastoral Vermont dirt road between the two locations, I only had one tape in the car, Bob Dylan's *Blood on the Tracks*. "Your gonna make me lonesome when you go," ricocheted between my head and heart as I watched Amy and Hali heroically remain positive and loving even as hope quickly evaporated. It was on those drives that I did my crying, because it was about the only spare time I had. By the end I was the general overseer on the jobsite and in charge of the memorial service as well. On Monday, July 29, 2002, Chris Bracken summoned the strength to come up to the house and sit for the first time and enjoy the view from his living room. As he looked out at the breeze ruffling through the pine and maple trees on the mountainside, he turned to Kevin and said, "I can't thank you enough. I worked my whole life so I could sit here and enjoy this view." We were all choked up, and Kevin tried to break the sobriety of the moment by saying, "Well, I don't know how we did it with a guy like this running the job," as he smiled and nodded at me. Chris said, "Yeah, a guy I can ask to do *anything* and he does it, that kind of guy," and he smiled and looked right at me as he said, "Thanks, Barry." That's how late it was, there was no more time for even good-natured put downs for Chris, just generosity, gratitude, and love. If I can be one-tenth as brave as he was when my time comes, I'll die a proud man.

The last time I ever saw Chris alive, he was too weak to do anything but say, "Can't talk." I reached over to hold his hand, and Chris somehow managed to change his position so that we were in the handshake rather than hand holding position. He couldn't talk, but he could still make a statement—friends shook hands. For the next ten minutes, while still gripping his hand, I took the chance to thank him for his wonderful friendship and to promise him that he would never be forgotten. His eyes would focus on me now and then and convey warmth. Finally I had to let his hand, and my friend, go.

A few hours later on Saturday, August 3, 2002, at around 4 PM Chris Bracken died, with Amy and his sister, Mary, at his side.

Kevin and I worked hard all day Sunday and Monday after Chris had passed; we wanted the visitors due for his service Tuesday to see the place at its best. Monday night I zipped up to Stowe and my friend Bob Hambrecht's (a great boyhood pal from my hometown. Skaneateles. New York) for a shower and the use of his computer, so that I could compose some thoughts about Chris. Throughout the ordeal Bob gave me the run of his place for whatever I needed as well as emotional support and generous portions of wisdom. My sister Mary Jo, who has worked with the terminally ill for years, called regularly to prepare me for what was to come and to suggest comforts that would soothe Chris. My longtime love interest, Karen Crist, handled everything at home without a complaint so that I could drop our life to do what needed to be done. The person with whom Chris and I always spent the most time and had the most laughs, our dear pal Ian Baston, sent me money that helped save the project the week before Chris died. He has dug into his wallet again and again since then.

Chris Bracken's family and friends held a beautiful memorial service for him on Wednesday, August 7, in the Barnard, Vermont, town hall. We laughed and cried as we remembered him. We hovered around Amy and Hali and Chris's mother, Verna; his brother, Denis; his uncle, Carroll Miles; his sister-in-law, Rhonda; his niece, Elizabeth; and his nephew, Simon, as if the proximity of our compassion could somehow salve such a cruel wound. Our hearts were knitted together in love and anguish. True to Chris's nature, the memorial service wasn't dogmatic or stodgy. One of his best friends, Chuck Gunderson, served as the gracious, eloquent, and warm master of ceremonies. Several of his other best friends spoke from the heart with wit and love. Hali and Elizabeth did a reading of Bernie Taupin's lyrics from "Your Song," changing the tense at the end of the refrain to "when you were in the world." They were great. Finally another of his best friends—me—formally eulogized Chris Bracken.

We had a reception that took place in the hall following the service. As I spoke with all the mourner-celebrants, it struck me how profoundly the world had been changed by the loss of this one good person. Everyone's heart was broken. Everyone was flabbergasted that a forty-eight-year-old very fine man could be stolen so quickly. Everyone was scared by life's random brutality and indifferent cruelty. Everyone wished that there was some way to take on even more pain if it could relieve Amy and Hali and his family of just a little of their own.

And then, after a few more days on the house project, I found myself back home in upstate New York, trying to return to my work, which entails paying close attention to people like George W. Bush.

It's been a tough adjustment, particularly now that I am in possession of the all-too-costly perspective that the loss of a dear and vital loved one provides. Chris always referred to W. as the "MOE-RON," which rolled off his tongue with the eloquent impatience of a person who had grown up in Northern New Jersey traffic. Upon my return, Bush seemed more MOE-RONIC than ever—especially since all he has done for the past several weeks is froth at the mouth over Saddam Hussein. He says he wants a regime change, but what he really wants is the world's second-largest oil reserve, and he is willing to send American troops into combat to secure it. He is doubly willing to massacre scores of Iraqi peasants under the guise of saving them.

And that's why my new and awful perspective costs me sleep. I had just spent the summer in an intimate and dreadful embrace with mortality. After seeing Chris fight with literally everything he had to remain part of this world, I had renewed respect for life, at least in part because I had a closer understanding of death. No matter how we try, we can't stop the grim reaper from making his appointed rounds. All the good medicine, good intentions, and love in the world can't keep each of our numbers from eventually coming up. Until then we will have to live through the gradual loss of most of the people we have ever known and cared for. At forty-nine, I can no longer count all the friends I have lost. All four of my grandparents, my father, and my dear, sweet infant nephew Gavin have now been gone for years. I'm very sentimental. I still miss every one of my dogs, who lived their lives at an extremely unfair seven-times-human speed. Lost, Fluke, Zack, and Keed all haunt me, as does Chris's dog, Larry. She had to be put down because of extreme old age (fifteen) just at the time Chris was originally diagnosed with cancer. I had named her. (Chris called and asked for suggestions but didn't specify a gender. "Okay," he said, "her name is Larry.")

My current hound, Lloyd, and I now wander the New York countryside that I left lush and green in July but that had time-lapsed into a dry and multicolored burst of wildflowers and leaves during my absence. Fall is ripe with melancholy this year. I walk back inside, turn on the computer or worse, the television, where the cable news networks clamor for war in hopes of a payoff during October ratings sweeps. There are heartening amounts of broad-based opposition to W's bloodlust for Iraq, but the Democrats look like they aren't about to do much to represent that widespread view. After attending to some mere formalities at the UN, where the rest of the world has clearly taken up Bush's offer to decide if it was "with us or against us" by choosing the latter, he will unleash holy hell on the Iraqi people. It won't matter that he has been caught in lie after lie while rattling his red-white-and-blue saber. He has his heart set on war, and like the spoiled rich brat that he is, he'll whine until he gets his way.

We all did everything we could to save Chris Bracken, but sadly, his death was unavoidable. Right now, in far-off Iraq, thousands face even more senseless deaths as the United States prepares to set a synthetic grim reaper in motion. And good people, who just happen to speak a different language, wear different clothes, and live under a different illegitimate leader than did Chris Bracken, are going to die. The ripple effect of those deaths will bring unavailing grief to their loved ones, just as grief engulfed Chris's survivors. And they will hate the United States as Chris's survivors hate liver cancer. The only difference between their grief and ours is that liver cancer, the cause of our anguish, couldn't have been stopped if the American people rose up and spoke out against it with righteous indignation.

And so, at the end of heartbreaking and weary months, I sit and wonder when it will be that my country will gather the courage to become morally superior to liver cancer. As it stands, it would be a marked improvement if the USA were merely to become its moral equal. As we sat at that memorial service in Vermont last summer, we didn't have to worry about liver cancer returning and carpet-bombing those of us who survived its cruel theft of life.

Liver cancer may have destroyed the dream Chris had of moving into his new house with Amy and Hali, but it didn't destroy the house, much less all the other houses and towns and cities in the area. But make no mistake, that's exactly what George Bush is asking us to endorse: the massacre of innocents and the destruction of all that people need to get by each day. He'll tell us that we must strike to keep Hussein from using chemical weapons. He won't mention that the United States will surely destroy Iraq's sewer systems, thus causing cholera and other epidemics and many more horrifically painful and needless deaths. He will invoke 9/11 and a commitment to fight terrorism, while surrounding himself with retro-terrorist bureaucrats like Richard Armitage (deputy secretary of state and current roving minister of doom), Elliott Abrams (who has some bogus National Security Council title concerning democracy), John Negroponte (UN ambassador), John Poindexter (who came and went from his job at the now officially defunct but definitely looming Total Information Awareness project}, and so many more who engineered the United States–backed death-squad activity that lethally intimidated the peasants of Central America back when Bush's poppy was vice-president. He'll wrap his intentions in the flag as he wipes his ass with the Bill of Rights. He'll tell us the sky is about to fall unless there is a regime change, and he'll equate Saddam Hussein with Hitler. But *he* will be the one who has sent troops all over the globe, driven by dreams of world domination. That thug Hussein would love to do the same, but as a world-beater he's a piker compared to Bush and his carnivorous handlers.

One day, near the end, Chris and I flipped on CNN for a moment, just as George W. Bush was walking toward a podium with body language that announced he was about to start lying well before he began to speak. Chris said, "Arggh, the MOE-RON! Make it stop, make it stop!"

I extinguished the television and Chris said, "Thanks. There are still some things that are worse than liver cancer."

Exactly, my friend. Exactly.

2002 Cont'd

The subtle yet inimitable influence of Henry Kissinger permeated news that the Pentagon had secret plans for nuking seven nations. Energy secretary Spencer Abraham privately hoped Bush would drop the Big One on the Middle East so that we could begin burning nuclear-fossil fuels. Kaiser Ashcroft doesn't think of them as nukes—he considers them "rapture accelerants."

In the Middle East, Israel seized more land because Palestinian suicide bombers struck again because Israel began construction on a fence because Palestinian suicide bombers struck again because Israel launched rocket attacks because Palestinian suicide bombers struck again because Israel bulldozed occupied homes because Palestinian suicide bombers struck again because Israel leveled neighborhoods . . .

In response, Bush admonished Yasir Arafat to resume "security cooperation" against terrorism with Israel. Security cooperation between Ariel Sharon and Arafat was about as likely as a poison-control program between cobras.

In the beginning, there were priests and they saw that the collar was good . . . for covering up what they did with what was under the rest of their robes. By April, many American Catholics began kicking themselves for not questioning those NAMBLA *Journal* inserts in the Sunday Bulletin.

In May, Bush administration officials said that the new International Criminal Court would get no cooperation from the United States—outside of necessitating it.

In light of the upcoming ban on soft money in federal elections, a spring Republican corporate fundraiser was the equivalent of throwing a keg party at the entrance to an AA meeting.

As the first post-9/11 Memorial Day approached, New York City was singled out for several color-coded warnings. This blatantly political diversion was akin to yelling, "Priest!" in a roomful of altar boys.

In late June, President Bush underwent a colonoscopy, during which doctors successfully located his head, but only after performing an emergency procedure to remove the entire Fox News Network.

Voting irregularities in the Democratic gubernatorial primary invoked the six scariest words in American politics: *Florida is back in the news.*

An interesting statistical truth was learned in 2002: The same people who calculate royalties for record companies work weekends estimating the size of crowds at peace rallies, and the crowd estimates never include the FBI agents.

October ended with the horrible news of the deaths of Senator Paul Wellstone, his wife Sheila, his daughter Marcia, three staff members, and two pilots in a small-plane crash in Minnesota. Wellstone had composed about 60 percent of all the great people in the Senate.

Osama bin Laden is like Jimi Hendrix. Nobody has seen the guy in ages, but his new recordings just keep coming out, including a new release in time for the holidays.

five

Lousy Corporate Homogenization

O ver the years many people have attempted to disarm me by asking: Is there *anything* you like? Hey, I love doing what I do, which is to say I love taking on big targets. In my work as a stand-up comic I've always hated listening to comedians whose stock-in-trade is belittling the weak and defenseless. Two things have saved me from the bitterness that engulfs many comedians. First is my ability to deal with plagiarists. I used to get ripped off a lot, and it drove me crazy. Then one day I realized I should simply write and perform material *I wanted repeated*, and it made all the difference. At best a good message gets spread, at worst I'm not ripped off. Second and most important was finding a context for my work. I have seen some wonderful and brilliant acts become huge and deserving comedy stars. I have watched some real lowlifes also become successful and wealthy beyond imagination. It took me time to realize that this is as it has always been. The difference between the true greats and the second-rates is that although both can do well during contemporary times, only the greats' work will stand the test of time.

For me it always comes back to my friend Twain. He wrote things a hundred years ago that most people wouldn't dare sign today. Those writings have sustained me through the darkest of political times. I'd like to leave something that someone might find one day, when they needed to learn they weren't the first person to feel a certain way. I will never reach a small fraction of the people that Clemens still does, but someday, somewhere, a person might find my work and see in it a thoughtful resistance to the madness of an era. It may encourage that person to do the same during some distant difficulties. I always try to write with that person in mind.

I've also always done a lot of what is called preaching to the choir. I don't apologize for this since the choir in America really needs a night out every now and then. The choir is made up of the best people in the world, the kind of people who will hold a sign that says, "No War," even when every TV newscast is nothing short of a pep rally for carnage. They are the kind of people who wear pins that reflect their humanity rather than their nationality. And they take lonely and brave stands. So what I do is never "just" preaching to the choir because preaching to the choir, is an essential task. Its ranks include courageous and weary sweethearts who will leave my performance reenergized if I do my job well. Much the same as you never hear a misogynist comic called political, you rarely hear all the inveighing that reinforces American mainstream wrong-headedness as preaching to the choir. Well, their choir is a lot bigger than mine, and there are few complaints about the nature of their sermons. I will always perform anywhere that meets some very basic physical and artistic standards. I know how to approach most any assemblage. I have done hundreds of shows for very mainstream audiences, and those appearances have almost always gone just fine; in fact, they have often helped increase the size of the proverbial choir.

The choir needs to know that they are not alone and that at times *it really is the world that is crazy*. The simple act of sending out a response to one of Bush's speeches provoked several people to e-mail their gratitude. They added color and detail to the Bush indictment, meant to assist me in my next assault. That's pretty goddamned great. I scratched an itch in my own soul and by doing so, brought relief to many. In turn they have broken the conspiracy of silence so vital to petty little tyrannies and thereby strengthened our cause by speaking up and spreading the message. They will take all of our words out into the world with them. As voices grow louder, the conspiracy of silence weakens. This is happening at this very moment with the antiwar movement. Back when Dubyahoo's Daddy was elected-President Bush, it was much harder to organize people. But then the greedheads messed up. After decades of selling us mountains of trash we never needed, they sold us some valuable devices: computers, modems, and digital cameras. We can use these tools to record, comment on, and change history.

In the past the only voice we heard was that of AUTHORITY. It was patriarchal and final. Far too often the proclamations emanated from a big mouth on a head with no ears. Its eyes were extremely hampered by tunnel vision. To make ourselves feel a bit safer, we have often worshiped that voice. We still do. It makes us feel better to think, "If Al Gore were president, things would be OK." Well, things would be better, no doubt about it. The actual winner of the election would hold his rightful office and that would be nice. And he probably wouldn't be putting Klan sympathizers on the federal bench nor would he have corporate lobbyists writing environmental law, two distinct advantages over the current regime.

But here's the thing: if we continue to base our lives around the search for a president, then we can't get much else done. So I don't need, to borrow a phrase from the late sportswriter Red Smith, god-up politicians. If politicians are involved, then so are bad compromises. Progressives must get out and effect as much change as possible and make our presence known; then, when election time comes around, perhaps a few politicians will see the percentage in leaning just a skosh our way. Of course everyone everywhere will work hard down the stretch in 2004 to turn out the vote to turn Bush out of office. Come election day, we'll know which compromise we must make. It just seems insane to waste our entire lives thinking strictly in terms of it.

Just because I am a critic doesn't mean I'm a negative person. I don't think negative people try to change the world for the better. I think it would be fair to call me a sentimental skeptic. Skaneateles kids love lots of stuff. We loved the lake we grew up on. We loved playing sports and rooting for nearby Syracuse University in football, basketball, and lacrosse. We loved rock and roll and partying. We loved our friends, we loved our town, and we loved our families. Most of all, we loved to laugh.

If it weren't for the lake, I wouldn't have become an environmentalist. If it weren't for sports, I wouldn't have become a proponent of civil rights. If it weren't for rock and roll and the people I met partying, I'd never have opened my mind to a world much different from the one in which I grew up.

If it weren't for laughter, I'd never have found my place on the fringes of society.

Ronald Reagan: "I will not negotiate with terrorists—either they take the weapons or they don't. These prices are firm!"

I don't like Florida, I have a problem with any state where the electric chair only goes to "medium high."

When I mentioned that I had done several AIDS benefits, some of my old hometown acquaintances pulled me aside and asked, "You're not a queer, are you?"

I replied, "I'm whatever threatens you. I'm a Communist with AIDS, and I bite!"

Sure, John Kerry can bring out Green Berets he saved in Nam, but you never hear about the several times Bush took the wheel when his guardsmen buddies were too hammered to drive. Yup, old W was the best damned shit-faced driver in his battalion, but he'd never stoop to exploiting it for political purposes.

If they gave out purple hearts for hangovers, W would have been the most decorated soldier of the Vietnam era.

six

Encounters with
National Plutocrat Radio

Two years into the court-appointed Bush administration's destruction of our way of life I received a call from NPR with a request to *belittle Democrats*. A producer for a show called *On Point* wanted me to make fun of the fact that the field of Democratic candidates for the presidency had grown very quickly in recent weeks. That's right, NPR was soliciting me to satirize democracy for showing signs of vibrancy. And so this young producer tried to steer me that way. She started by mentioning the size of the Democratic field and then asked, "Do you think any of them has the stature to take on George W. Bush?"

I said, "My dog Lloyd has the stature to take on Bush." But then I allowed, "Of course, I raised him myself."

We went back and forth, and I said I could run down the field for her. She reminded me twice that the game I was to bag was of the Democratic variety. I said I'd put something together for her. I requested a list of candidates in case I'd overlooked someone. She sent the Dem roster, and the next morning, I wrote the piece. They had my script by midday Wednesday. I was supposed to tape it Thursday. I figured if I got it in early, we could sort out any difficulties with time to spare. Like I said, I'm a professional.

It wasn't bad for short notice. It was about as innocuous as I can be while retaining the rights to my soul. I did make it clear that I thought the sheer volume of candidates was a good thing. But it had good jokes about all the candidates without cutting a millimeter of slack for Bush. It also made it clear that I thought the size of the field was an indication of political health and W's vulnerability.

I didn't hear anything from *On Point* that afternoon. Early in the evening I got an e-mail from the producer (or assistant or whatever she is) telling me that another person (and I am withholding the names of these people as a courtesy to youth) would "give you a call tomorrow morning to go over the piece with you. Thanks for getting it to us so promptly. We've been a little swamped today on this end."

I knew this meant trouble. "Go over it with you" was the key phrase. It meant "scrap and rewrite."

I waited around all morning—no calls. I had other pressing matters to attend to. Nevertheless, as a writer-performer I am hardwired to get one task done at a time. And so from Tuesday evening until Thursday afternoon I was distracted by this radio essay. It promised to pay only a measly $100, but hey, I'm an artist, and money isn't my primary concern.

Finally, at 12:15 PM my promised morning call arrived. A producer, this time a young man, started with tepid praise but then told me that what was really wanted was a "satire" on the size of the field. He said this as if I somehow couldn't understand the word *satire*. He sold his point by using exaggerated emphasis, as if I needed help grasping the concept that he thinks it's silly for so many candidates to be in the running for the Democratic bid. "There are *three new ones this week*! When will it end??!!" He was confident at first, but that didn't last long. I can be rather difficult, particularly when I'm right.

I said I wasn't the person to write this "satire" because I was encouraged by the size of the field. It demonstrated that pols have been emboldened by the grassroots opposition to Bush. The millions in the streets have translated into more choices for president because the GOP's bloated and soft underbelly was hanging over its pants. It means the field isn't being prematurely narrowed, thereby excising important views before the public can vote on them. It is good in a democracy when there are a lot of candidates. I said I wouldn't sanitize wrong-headed conventional wisdom by making it "wacky."

I continued by saying that if they think the broadening field is something to belittle, then they really don't possess much political sophistication. A broad field is an indication that the possibilities aren't about to be narrowed, thus making it easier for the moneyed few to buy all the viable candidates.

I made a point of telling this fellow that I understood that it was just his bad luck to have caught the assignment of dealing with me and that this was nothing personal. I actually felt sorry for the guy. He had one trump card—he could either put me on the air or not. I quickly tore it to pieces by making it crystal clear that they could put their show in an NPR tote bag and place it somewhere far removed from solar occurrences. I told him that their money ($100!!) was worth neither my time nor talent. I would read the essay I wrote and even clean it up a bit, if they liked. But I had neither the time nor inclination to turn it into something in which I did not believe. He said I didn't understand. They weren't looking for "commentary," they wanted "satire." Besides, this was a segment called "Radio Diaries" and not meant for commentary. There were plenty of other places to do that on NPR. (Oh yeah, they're calling me *all* the time!) He said they didn't really want a rundown of the candidates. Well then, why the question of "stature"? And why e-mail me the list of Dems with hats in or near the ring? Besides, to make fun of the field of candidates for its sheer size *would be commentary.* Hell, *all satire is commentary.* And *that's what I do, ask around. I am a commentator.* Having run dangerously low on italics, I was happy our call was nearly over.

He said that he would talk to his senior producer and promised to get back to me "one way or the other." He never did.

I wish I had read the On Point website before speaking with this person. I'd have quoted its description of what Radio Diaries are: "These personal essays written and narrated by listeners allow fresh voices and fascinating viewpoints to be heard on public radio . . ."

Bush's Mars exploration plans represent some serious foresight. One day this Iraq boondoggle will end and Halliburton will need something like a Mars mission for fleecing the taxpayer.

Of course it will take a lot of R&D dollars for Halliburton to determine how to bribe microbes on Mars.

W is pushing education as a campaign theme this year. OK, technically it's "reeducation" for registered Democrats—nevertheless, he's pushing it.

Bush says he is eating beef and isn't vaguely concerned about the possibility of mad cow disease. Of course he isn't—the disease attacks *the brain*.

seven

Phil, Ralph, and the Mick

I have loved the New York Yankees my entire life. I've listened to, watched, or found some way to be updated on the scores of nearly every Yankee game since the 1960 season. That was the year I made my First Communion and received a transistor radio from my parents in honor of the occasion. My father, Philip Owen Crimmins, was a traveling salesman and I had three sisters and no brothers. With Dad so frequently on the road, that radio became a large part of my connection with the male world. My mother, the former Margaret Mary Donovan, a champion on ski slopes and golf links, never lost the baseball fever with which her father, a Dodgers fan, had imbued the young Margaret Mary Donovan. She spent patient hours hitting my bat with the ball so that I could gain the confidence necessary to become athletically adept.

Dad had been jilted by our national pastime, having been a boyhood supporter of the Boston Braves. His devotion did not make the move to Milwaukee with the franchise. Even when he was home, I spent a lot of time alone with the Yankees and their broadcasters. My hero of heroes was, not surprisingly, Mickey Mantle. By 1968 that radio was in worse shape than the Mick's perennially injured knees, its black plastic cracked, gold speaker mesh dented, and the clip-on battery cover longer gone than any of Mantle's tape-measure homers. But like Mickey, the radio always came through in the clutch.

The first year I made a trip to Yankee Stadium was 1968. On August 25, 1996, I returned to that noble edifice for the unveiling of the first new monument in the Stadium since the 1940s. It commemorates the late, great Mickey Mantle.

I had seen the Yanks on family vacations in Boston a couple of times and in Cooperstown for the Hall of Fame Game but had waited forever, a lifetime, to go to the Stadium. Finally on a late June day just prior to my fifteenth birthday, my ordeal was about to end. My father and I arose at 5:00 AM so that we could make the six-hour drive from our home in Skaneateles, New York, to see the Yankees play the Detroit Tigers. Somehow Dad had acquired mezzanine box tickets, which in the old ballpark were the poshest of the posh. Gorgeous weather accompanied us as we wound our way from the idyllic rolling hills of Central New York to the most prominent pasture of all in the Bronx. As we rounded a curve on the Major Deegan Expressway, Yankee Stadium materialized. It was even more imposing than I had imagined. It was massive, stately, historic, majestic. Most importantly, it was the home of the Yankees, and somewhere inside Mickey Mantle was being mummified with tape in preparation for the game I was about to see. I told myself then and there that when I grew up, I would not be a stranger to these surroundings. As we pulled down the ramp and looked for a parking space, I never broke eye contact with the magnificent structure, fearing that if I let it out of my sight, I might have had to wait another fourteen years before it appeared again.

Upon parking Dad's 1965 Chrysler wagon, we ambled through the shadows of the Stadium to Manny's Baseball Land. I had learned of Manny's and become a faithful customer through ads that appeared in various baseball publications. For years I had dreamed of the day I could go into his "Land" and browse for hours and buy all of the memorabilia I wanted. Maybe I would even meet and become close with Manny, from whom I would be able to score great Yankee tickets. But throughout the Land, Manny was nowhere to be found. There wasn't room for him. Manny's Land turned out to

be a literal hole in the wall. My first experience at his diminu-
tive establishment consisted of purchasing a *1968 Yankee Year-
book* from a decidedly disinterested clerk.

I recovered quickly from my disillusionment; nothing could ruin
this day for me. As we walked toward the ballpark, it got larger
and larger, and I cranked my neck back further and further,
mouth wide open. I was in full tourist gawk. We strolled into
Yankee Stadium via the entrance that was especially for members of the Stadium Club. The tickets we had belonged to some
corporation and were season seats, which permitted us into the
Club, which seemed to me the most exclusive restaurant in the
world. Once inside, I absorbed a lot more of my surroundings
than my lunch—the place was a miniature Hall of Fame.

After eating, I was absolutely beside myself with anticipation.
Dad paid the tab, and finally we headed inside the ballpark. Our
seats were at press box level, between home plate and the visiting
dugout. The Stadium more than delivered on its exterior promises. It was lush and green, and there were a humongous score
board and electronic-message board. Public-address announcer
Bob Sheppard's dignified voice boomed clearly, and I could
understand every word he said. The mezzanine box seats were
comparable to those found in a movie theater. There were even
waitresses. This was tremendous!

Unfortunately all of the baseball we saw at Yankee Stadium
that day consisted of this: Yankee utility infielder Ruben Amaro
playing catch with the batboy in what was quickly becoming a
torrential downpour. When the game was canceled forty-five
minutes later (that was made up in a weekend series with Detroit,
during which Rocky Colavito, an outfielder, *pitched* and won for
the Yanks!), I was inconsolable. I'd waited my entire childhood
to see the Yanks play at the Stadium, to see the Mick hit a homer
in the Bronx. Instead, I got to see *Ruben Amaro play catch with
a batboy.* As we slumped out onto the soggy streets, I made sure

that my father understood how much I appreciated his heroic efforts to get me to the park and obtain such premium tickets. But on the long ride home I went into a deep depression that was to last for quite a while. I was never going to get to see the Yanks play at the Stadium. Worse, the Mick was in the twilight of his career, and if I ever did get back, he might be gone.

On a Friday night some weeks later I bounced home, buoyed by a victory by my summer baseball team. I was going to catch a quick shower and head to the movies with some my teammates. There were vague plans to meet up with some girls. I was coming out of my funk. As I stepped out of the shower, my father pounded on the door and said, "Ralph Cheche [pronounced "Checky"] is on the phone, and he wants to talk to you."

This was odd. Ralph Cheche was my father's friend, and he had never called me before. I loved him because he was funny, and when he was around, my father was always in a better mood. Dad, you see, often had a demeanor not unlike that of Bob Dole. Impatient WWII guy stuff. Ralph was a Korean War veteran. While overseas, he had contracted a bizarre condition that had caused him to lose all of the hair on his body. He resembled a hairless, somewhat more svelte version of the insult comic Jack E. Leonard. I had traveled with my father and Ralph to numerous Syracuse football games and several Sports Smokers—fundraising events that inevitably featured a speech from some sports luminary and plenty of second-hand smoke for fans of all ages. We had seen Yogi Berra at one such gathering and legendary football coach Paul Brown at another the previous winter. We had also gone to four or five Army-Navy games over the years with Ralph. Outside of making it to Yankee Stadium, I had not been deprived of many sporting events.

I grabbed the phone and said hello. Ralph asked me what I was doing that weekend. I mentioned a yardwork job that I had to finish either Saturday or Sunday.

Ralph Cheche said, "Finish it Sunday. We are going to a ball game tomorrow."

I answered, "Great. Who's playing?"

He asked, "If you could see anyone play tomorrow, who would you like to see?"

I replied, " Well I guess the Syracuse Chiefs [the local minor league baseball team], but they play tomorrow night. I could still work and go to the game."

Ralph said, "If you could see *anyone*, it would be the Syracuse Chiefs? Well, I guess you wouldn't be that interested in going to New York to see the Yankees. What if I told you it was Old-Timers Day? My brother and I have an extra ticket and thought you might want to join us, but if you really want to see the Chiefs . . ."

I responded with great urgency, "What time do we leave Mr. Cheche?!!"

Ralph answered, "I'll pick you up about 8:00 A M."

"But Mr. Cheche, it's a day game. We could never get to Yankee Stadium in time if we drive down that late."

"That's why we are taking my brother's plane," said Ralph, no longer suppressing a laugh that was genuine and kind.

All I could utter was, "Wow. We'll be ready. Thanks, Mr. Cheche."

But *we* didn't need to be ready. My father claimed he was busy and couldn't make it. But Ralph only had one extra ticket—a seat he doubtless offered his dear friend, my father, first. But Dad must have told Ralph to take me instead. Phil Crimmins had always given me a hard time about rooting for the Yanks, but I know he was glad for me that I had found a rightful place as a booster of the greatest franchise in history. That day my father passed up his trip to Old-Timers Day so that I could attend the game. He never once implied that he had any interest in going, but upon my return his cross-examination of me about every detail indicated otherwise.

We flew into Teterboro, New Jersey, and parked our plane right next to Frank Sinatra's Lear Jet (!) We got a cab and headed for the Ballyard in the Bronx. The sun shone brightly all day. It sparkled on the Stadium, on the Old-Timers, on Mickey Mantle's two homers, on Stan Bahnsen's brilliant pitching performance, and it particularly shined on Ralph Cheche's bald head. The Yanks lost 3–2. Mickey accounted for all of the New York scoring with his home runs. It was the last time he would ever hit two in one game. I had gotten back just in time; Mickey Mantle retired from baseball the following spring.

After the contest, we went to Manhattan to get some dinner, and when we came outside, it was overcast and foreboding. Mr. Cheche's brother made a call to some official weather place and it was decided that we should spend the night, since flying would be dangerous. Inclement weather, my nemesis just a few weeks earlier, had become my ally. I was going to spend the night in New York! After we checked into a hotel, Ralph took me on a cab tour of Manhattan. That evening we went to see some long-forgotten singer in a nightclub, where Ralph was welcomed like a long-lost relation. I was living it up with the boys in the Big Apple! We had a great night recounting our various trips to other events and discussing the great Yankee teams of the past and many of the players we had seen that day. Nobody suggested we stay for the game the next day and I certainly knew it would have been inappropriate to lobby for more baseball. But the thought crossed my mind.

We got up early the next morning and flew back under ideal conditions. That afternoon as I weeded, clipped, mowed, and trimmed, I listened to the Yanks get trounced by Minnesota 11–2. As bad as the game was, I paid attention to every pitch. I felt much more a part of things now, even as the Yanks were losing their fifth in a row. Hey, it was a losing streak, but damn it, I was involved.

In the past few years Mickey Mantle, Ralph Cheche, and Phil Crimmins have all passed away. I have grown up and worked in show business for almost a quarter-century. Sometimes my connections are even better than Ralph Cheche's or my father's. I have been fortunate enough to obtain tickets and special access for many people to lots of events. They often say, "You don't know how much this means to us."

I just smile and think back to my father, Ralph Cheche, Mickey Mantle, and the summer of 1968 and say, "I bet I do."

Dennis Miller's new show debuts on CNBC on Monday, and if all goes well, a slot on Bloomberg isn't out of the question. *Just what America needs: a smug quisling mugging above its stock quotes.*

Pretty soon Miller will be doing shows in the exciting new smaller portion of the "picture in picture" format on a public-access cable show near you.

To sell out *that much* and still end up on CNBC is just pitiful.

eight

The Rushmore of Wrong-Headedness

I used to write for Dennis Miller in 1992, when he had a syndicated talk show. During the program's one season Miller went from endorsing Jerry Brown to becoming a big Ross Perot supporter. A political impulse buyer, his ideological cannon was never lashed very securely to the deck. Over the years that cannon somehow became lodged on the starboard side of the vessel. Each time Miller receives a paycheck, he seems to take it to a bank further to the right of the last one. And now, more than a decade since I wrote my last joke for the man, I can only watch in stupefaction as this once hip and inside comic completes his transformation into a lout whose act sounds as if it were ghostwritten by George Jessel. Actually, that's not fair . . . to George Jessel.

Dennis Miller was always decent to me. He gave me a chance, and I appreciated it, but he has become so obstinately wrong of late that I am left with no choice but to comment.

His attempt to style himself as a Hollywood rebel by completely sucking up to the ultimate "suits"—which is to say the ones in Washington—is self-aggrandizing and pitiful. But then, tough as he speaks, Miller never met a powerful or connected guest he didn't suck up to. So it's predictable that he would court the braying repressionists who have seized control of the White House. Now we must listen to Miller blather insufferably as he refers with devotion to George W. Bush with the ever-possessive term "my president." After all, we are expected to surmise, W must be good if he belongs to that self-styled Hollywood rebel Dennis Miller! Right? Miller is so egotistical that he thinks that by referring to Bush again and again as "my president," he somehow legitimizes W's odious path to 1600 Pennsylvania Avenue. He believes his verbal consecration will make us forget that the little bastard stole the White House. To do otherwise would be to risk having Dennis Miller label us un-hip. Heaven forfend!

No longer the youthful and sassy anchor of *SNL*'s "Weekend Update" of all those years ago, Miller has become a national father figure. And what a lousy dad he is. Listening to his act is no longer something we look forward to; it is more like getting stuck in the back seat of your pop's station wagon while he lectures you on "Americanism" through thirty miles of heavy traffic. In front of your friends.

But give Miller credit; he has accomplished something that almost no one before him has ever been able to do. He has actually become so vile that he is not suitable company even in *Hollywood*. He can now make a game-show host shudder in revulsion. This works well for the self-involved Miller. Why waste time considering the true horror and long-term ramifications of the violence he so blindly supports, when we could instead be focusing on the assault of cold shoulders he has sustained on Rodeo Drive? Yeah, Dennis, enough of this massacre-of-innocents stuff, let's talk about *you*.

As cocksure as Miller is in his new political alliance, he'd better watch himself—he could be headed toward a twenty-first-century version of Hitler's Night of the Long Knives. So long as church-state integrationist John Ashcroft is the attorney general, a purge of the potty-mouthed comic is never a distant possibility.

The beauty of Dennis Miller is that everything he's saying is on tape. It will be available for review by people for a long, long time. He has carved a place for himself on the Mount Rushmore of wrong-headedness, and there he will stay for years to come, a glowering, reactionary oaf for the ages. He's ready for his close-up, Mr. Murdoch.

Marijuana is a very dangerous drug. Some people smoke it just once and go directly into politics.

The Pentagon's so greedy it has an extra side on its building.

The Drug War—where Jim Crow meets Joe McCarthy.

The environment is screwed up, but you can still have fun. I'm going brown-water rafting this summer.

nine

Surfing the Niagara

onsidering my father's political conservatism and the rock-ribbed Republicanism of my hometown, I was an unlikely prospect to become a radical. Thankfully there were mitigating influences, like my mother and her father, Walter J. Donovan, an attorney from Massachusetts. We were visiting my grandfather at his rural summer residence in Savoy, Massachussets, during the 1960 Democratic National Convention. My father and Granddad took issue after issue with one another throughout the proceedings. In this generational dispute the elder man was the progressive, a lifelong Massachusetts Democrat with connections in Jack Kennedy's organization. Dad was the reactionary. Even at the age of seven I was well aware of his views.

I was supposed to be asleep during the Dem evening sessions, brought to us in fuzzy black and white by Chet Huntley and David Brinkley from the Los Angeles Sports Arena. Instead I loomed near a cracked doorway and listened to both the debates between Democrats on the Zenith and the interparty squabble in the living room of the rickety old farmhouse. "I didn't fight in a war to listen to people speak like that about America," said Dad. "Well then, perhaps someone needed to explain the purpose we needed to defeat fascism," retorted Granddad.

The farm was purchased by Walter J. during the Depression as a hedge against the potential collapse of his law practice. He figured he could plant crops if all else failed. It never came to that. His firm, Donovan and O'Connor, thrives to this very day, and the farm has remained a Berkshire escape for the family for nearly seventy-five years. That summer farmer Donovan planted a crop of doubt in my seven-year-old mind. His views seemed more sensible than Dad's, and he expressed them calmly, as if they could withstand questions without the fortification of bombast. And my mother, although diplomatic, was clearly embarrassed by her husband's rather loutish views. Since the lawyer's arguments were the most persuasive, I became a JFK man that week.

That fall I volunteered to speak for Kennedy before Miss Cecora's second-grade class. After promising, at my mother's whimsically knowing suggestion, that Kennedy would be good for kids because he'd raise teachers' salaries, therefore putting them in a better mood, Kennedy won the Cecora straw poll. It was the only known victory by a Democrat in any Skaneateles precinct that year or in anyone's memory.

By 1964 my father had worn me down and I was out leafleting for Barry Goldwater. This political veer to the right lasted until mid-adolescence. I was held in place mostly by talk of "freedom-loving" and "democracy," but eventually I realized that Tom Paine and Richard Nixon had nothing in common. Besides, I had been politically galvanized by unlikely outside agitators—the Skaneateles Police Department. I never cared for authority, particularly if I judged it to be in the wrong. While I was still in my mid-teen years, the local cops, short on crime and criminals, decided that they had better crack down on hippies. I was hard to label as a teen, coming down on the kid continuum somewhere between jock and freak. It took a while, but eventually, as a result of the "bad company" I kept, I made the police hit list. It changes you to know there are people working night and day to put you and your friends in jail simply because you wanted to have a little fun between blizzards.

I loved rock and roll and it led me to the *bad company* of longhairs, pot-smokers, and other fringe elements. These were just kids I knew, and they certainly weren't up to anything nearly as bad as had been suggested in the rampant rumors about them. The police harassment was awful yet comical. It was based rather literally on the T V show *Dragnet*. One week Friday and Morgan found drugs hidden in a car's air filter. For the next several months anytime anyone under thirty was stopped by the S P D, off came the air filter. Once, when one of the cops was pissed at me for some real or imagined act of insolence, he hit me with a verbatim rap from the previous evening's episode of *Dragnet*. "Someday you're going to make a mistake, Crimmins, and when you do, I'm going to be *right there* to cram it down your throat!"

Too bad he didn't bother to check my pockets, because they contained enough contraband to cram me down the river for an extended stay. You see, I had most of the evidence my friends and I planned on burning at an Allman Brothers concert that night. Concerts to us were what riverboats had been to young Sam Clemens. They came rolling into Syracuse, Ithaca, Rochester, or Buffalo and suggested a larger world. It was daunting at first but inviting as hell for bored kids from upstate New York. All we had wanted to do was smoke a little pot and go see Jerry Garcia or Eric Clapton or Pete Townsend play the guitar. The cops created a situation where you had to risk your very freedom to pursue such a natural diversion, all while people we knew were being sent to Vietnam to die for our alleged liberty.

We loved going to shows and counted down each instant between when we purchased our tickets, often weeks in advance and the night of an event. The scene outside concerts was almost as great as the moment inside when the houselights went down and the roar went up. There was a counterculture, and it welcomed us. Better yet, there were lots of great women to meet, knowing hippie women, happy to teach an upstate plowboy the best secret of all—if you want women to like you, you should start by liking them. And they were likable as hell. Soon they had us listening to Joni Mitchell and Bob Dylan and Joan Baez, and the lyrics became as important as the guitar licks. In the us-versus-them world the cops seemed intent upon creating, the musicians and their fans were most definitely us.

It was a heavy time. There were always rumors of the DA's office having sealed drug indictments engraved with our names. It only fortified our resolve to never back down, we had been careful and really hadn't done anything too rash or indiscreet, and we certainly weren't drug dealers. In Skaneateles we were the Vietcong, indigenous operatives with an ingrained knowledge of how to move about unobserved through backyards, alleys, and parking lots, or in the winter, traveling via the ice on the lake. We weren't always so lucky. The worst came when my friend Paul Fleig ended up going to Attica for a lousy bag of reefer. They would have let him off had he finked on anyone. Of course he didn't. Paul's still one of my best friends, and despite his two-year scholarship from the state, he has always maintained the same high principles that sent him away in the first place.

Because they lied to us about pot, we moved on to psychedelic drugs, which were fun even though our use of them came when war, jail, and total social upheaval loomed and couldn't help but enter the mind-expanded mix.

When concerts were in Buffalo, we'd drop some acid or mescaline, and after the show ended, we'd take the remainder of our buzz to Niagara Falls. Back then the National Park Service had just cut off access to several islands on the American side of the Niagara River, just above our nation's preeminent precipice. The footpath along the shore met a side path to the bridge that led to the small islands on the river. An erstwhile park worker put up two posts and ran a chain between them. Dangling from the chain was a wood-burned lettered sign with a friendly warning that read something like, "Unsafe—Pedestrian Traffic Prohibited."

A simple step over the chain, and *voila* we had the world's most dramatic archipelago upon which to continue our adventures. *All that good feeling and somewhere to go.* The roar of the river soothed the ringing in our post-concert ears. It also precluded anyone back on shore overhearing us howl with delight. At times we'd literally island hop onto smaller and smaller pieces of land. One misstep and we'd have been plummeting over Niagara Falls. Eventually we'd all have our own little clumps of terra not so firma. We cackled and screamed and laughed so hard at the sheer magnitude of the experience. The frothing Niagara caused discernible tremors on our precociously precious chunks of turf. At times you'd hop to another island, in fear that your current locale was about to break off into snarly oblivion. It was a rush—squared.

We only did this a few times, but ever since it's a rare week in which I don't think back to all I felt and wondered on those nights as I pondered the future while negotiating a violent and uncertain present. As an indigenous operative, I learned long before *Apocalypse Now* that Charlie *did* surf. How else could he prepare to take difficult stands in momentous currents for the rest of his life?

There's a "struggle for the soul of the Republican Party"? What are they using? Tweezers and an electron microscope?

Pennsylvania Republican Senator Rick Santorum is a homophobe? This is nearly as shocking as the Trent Lott racist revelations of last year!

I completely support the move to get Santorum to resign. In fact I thought he should resign long before he formally confirmed that he was a subscriber to this specific bigotry.

There are a lot of bigots in America and there is room for all of them under the Republican tent.

Or . . .

People say Republicans don't believe in diversity, but that's silly, they hate *everyone*.

ten

Why Is That Man Named After a Lizard Goose-Stepping Across My Television?

In late 1992 I was diagnosed with hepatitis C. Being in a union, I had good health insurance—which was unfortunate, because this made me eligible to be experimented on by Western science with a hellish drug called interferon.

After six months of abject torture it became clear that the drug was doing no good. Its main side effect, the complete loss of the will to live, was becoming a bit of an impediment. I stopped the treatments and decided to seek alternative therapy.

The following January a wonderful herbal healer from Cleveland told me that for all intents and purposes I had the Reagan and Bush administrations in my liver and that I would probably feel much better if we dislodged them. She explained to me that the liver is where all anger and outrage end up. (She's right. The mere thought of former Reagan State Department thug Elliott Abrams sends a missile of pain through my poor overworked vital organ.) She told me to let go of politics for a year or so, and then we could see how I was feeling.

After a summer of carrot juice and herbs the phone calls from back East started. "Teddy's in trouble," I was told, "and Cuomo's in for a battle, too."

And I said, "Oh my, what a shame. But I'm on my break. Besides, I never worshiped those guys anyway."

"Do you know who they're running against?" they rejoined.

"Yeah, I know their names. I'm sure they're businessmen, fathers, Christians, All-American white guys who hate taxes and crime and lay all the blame for them at the feet of their liberal opponents. Avoid becoming preoccupied with them. I speak from personal experience: they are bad for your health."

By mid-August there was a baseball strike-lockout, and I didn't have much to do, so I resumed reading the papers. I was feeling much better.

By early September I was out doing some concert openings for Steven Wright. We performed for a number of weekends around the country. And as I tuned in the TV, I started to notice the same guy was running for office—everywhere. It didn't matter what market I was in; the campaign spots were virtually identical:

As a prosecutor, he put everyone in his entire county in jail. As a businessman, he knows everyone's out to get you. As a legislator, he wrote the law that makes it permissible for the police to search your underwear drawer any time they feel like it. He's the national chairman of the Turn-in-Your-Neighbor-for-a-Safer-America Program. He's the kind of man who wears a tie when he goes fishing. He hates anyone who's ever been on welfare. He's been endorsed by a broad coalition of citizens, including Charlton Heston, Pat Buchanan, Rush Limbaugh, and the Young Republican Aryan Youth Bund. Isn't it time we sent this mealy-mouthed weasel to work for us in Washington? On Election Day let your complete lack of self-esteem speak loud and clear. Vote for Joseph McCarthy the Zillionth. (Paid for by the Committee to Distract You From Who Really Owns This Little Bastard.)

And these were the *positive* spots.

I just kept asking myself, who the hell would vote for these clowns? The polls, the media, my sources told me: everybody. I held hope that this conventional wisdom couldn't be right. Plus, no one could estimate the biggest unknown in this election: how many Republicans would forget to vote in deference to Ronald Reagan. (I have it on good authority, by the way, that the Great Communicator meant to mail his Alzheimer's letter to America thirty years earlier, but it slipped his mind.)

I also wondered where these clone candidates were coming from. Before I found out, I learned where they were going: to the District of Columbia, to take over Congress. Not to mention several governor's mansions. Election night was gruesome. It called to mind that November night in 1984 when we never even found out what color the networks were planning to use for Fritz Mondale on the Electoral College map.

After the electoral carnage I began watching c-span as if I were peering into a security video camera in a high-crime area. This election has so emboldened the reactionaries that they are actually telling us in no uncertain terms what they are up to. And what they are about.

For starters, they are ungracious in defeat, ungracious in victory. Witness Oliver North (there's something familiar about that phrase) and Newt Gingrich. As a loser, North did not have the good grace to congratulate his opponent. As a winner, Gingrich attacked the Clintons as "counterculture McGoverniks." In that one little blast Newt revealed volumes.

Two days after he won the biggest victory of his political career, he chose to Red-bait the president of the United States by tying him to *George McGovern*! The first Republican Speaker of the House in forty years fully expected to destroy liberalism the way Senator Joseph McCarthy destroyed the left.

There is a myth in this country that McCarthyism was buried with the senator's alcohol-addled carcass. But it is just not true. McCarthyism fueled the cold war and, as a result, the arms race. Ironically, it also caused the biggest, most exorbitantly funded socialist program in history. It is called the Pentagon.

McCarthyism did irreparable damage to the country because it told an entire school of intellectually viable thought, *You are unwelcome here. Keep out.* Mention socialism, and it's to the margins with you. Banished from the debate because some right-wing, thought-controlling hate-monger said so. And the country has lost much as a result. Like national health care.

Under Gingrich's congressional rule we stood to lose what liberals brought to the table. Aid to Families with Dependent Children; the idea that people who behave antisocially may be rehabilitated; worker safety; product liability; living wages; unemployment benefits; public education; sane environmental standards: none of it is safe once "liberal" becomes a pejorative.

The Republicans' Contract with America set out to hasten that process. And they assembled the team to do it. It was known as the 104th Congress. Thirty-three of the seventy-four new Republican House members were those clones from the ads. I found out what spawned them: Newt Gingrich raised millions for GOPAC, a political-action committee that he runs. With GOPAC funds Gingrich recruited and trained dozens of Republican candidates. The training included a series of videos starring Newt, who explained the simple principles of liberal-baiting and character assassination.

I have been criticized many times for likening right-wingers in this country to fascists. People have told me they thought it excessive. At times perhaps it was. But in the days since the 1994 election it became obvious that *fascist* is a word that can be applied without inviting hyperbole.

Particularly with regard to Senator Jesse Helms, the morality fetishist from North Carolina. I believe he was absolutely sincere when he followed up statements that Bill Clinton wasn't "fit to be commander-in-chief" by suggesting that the president "better bring a bodyguard" if he visited any North Carolina military bases. Helms would have like nothing better than a coup d'état.

When Jesse wasn't busy sniffing toilet seats at the National Endowment for the Arts, he was generally found furthering the cause of any number of authoritarian despots. Although this may injure the feelings of a few members of El Salvador's Arena Party, Helms's all-time favorite totalitarian has to be General Augusto Pinochet of Chile.

Pinochet led the bloody 1973 coup that toppled democratically elected President Salvador Allende. After Chilean troops assassinated Allende (the junta maintained that he committed suicide, apparently by shooting himself in the back dozens of times), Pinochet seized control and stomped his fascist boot on the Chilean people for the next seventeen years. Brutal political prisons were the scenes of unspeakable torture. Thousands were killed. Many more were exiled. Pinochet's terrorism spread to the United States with the Washington car-bomb assassination of Chile's last legitimate envoy to the United States, Ambassador Orlando Letelier.

Helms was a true believer in Pinochet's deepest political conviction: "Democracy is the breeding ground of communism." He does not believe in democracy if it results in people doing something he disagrees with. That's why he digs censorship and dictatorships. That's why we'd better pay attention when he intimates that the president is unsafe while visiting U.S. military installations.

Helms's soulmate back then was Senator Phil Gramm of Texas. The day after the 1994 election Gramm said that Republicans' top priority was to fight crime. How? Prisons. Tough ones. Gramm said that we should grab criminals "by the throat" and put them away. For good measure he added, "We don't want to hear what their daddy done to them, either."

What a brutal person. What a brutal country. I have a very simple suggestion for improving the efficacy of American prisons. Enforce the law within their walls. In particular, work to end rape inside correctional institutions. A lot fewer vicious people will be released from them if we simply adopted that goal. I promise the streets will become immeasurably safer. That is my entire crime bill.

When Newt spoke of reasserting American values, his target audience was the traditional abusive white guy. (Not all white guys, just the several million abusive ones.) Actually, I am speaking of the cult of the abusive white guy. It does not necessarily break down along racial or gender lines. Because not everyone who subscribes to the cult of the abusive white guy is white or even a guy. For example, AWGs include Clarence Thomas, Mona Charen, Phyllis Schlafly. You get the idea. At this point in our history, for PR purposes, the cult of the AWG requires female and ethnically diverse collaborators. But space is limited. Sell out now. Basically, AWGs include anyone who, on the high end of the cultural spectrum, could eat a meal with William Bennett without gagging or, on the low end, discovered bookstores only as a result of Rush Limbaugh's literary efforts.

What traditional American values suggest to these people is a return to a status quo that always had them at the front of the line regardless of merit. AWGs require undue advantage for themselves and strict social order for everyone but them. Now that there are a few rules that the patriarchy must adapt to, we have hit the mother lode of moaning crybabies. Boo, hoo. My obscene profits have been reduced because of environmental standards. Wahhhh. I can't leer at the women in my office anymore. Sniffle, sniffle. No ethnic jokes in the lunchroom.

Newt's message? *What I say goes. You women quiet down and get some food on the table, you shiftless Negroes get to work, you environmental nuts unhand industry. We have armaments to mass-produce. Now everyone pray on cue, and thank God for our return to morality.*

Term limits are a big part of the Contract with America. I must say, the idea of posting a congressional check-out time is inviting. I shed no tears for the 1994 loss of Dan Rostenkowski, Jim Sasser, and numerous others. Good riddance, cheesy bagmen. Term limits, scandal, whatever it takes to eliminate the hacks, it matters not.

Gingrich sold us the good old days—for the good old boys. Which is precisely why we should never return to them. I don't think you can find a time in U.S. history that many indigenous people would care to return to. I suspect there is no era that African-Americans would care to revive. Travel a fairly short distance in reverse, and women would lose the vote and much, much more. Head backward, and gays and lesbians would return to exceedingly more dangerous days.

In 1994 most voters didn't really want to go back. They just wanted change. Unfortunately there was very little choice. This government seemed to go in only two directions: nowhere and reverse. So reverse it was.

In my lifetime American voters have been all over a very small map. The Republicans were dead in 1964. Then the Dems in 1972. Each allegedly deceased party took the White House in the very next election. George Bush had a 90-plus percent approval rating during the Gulf War and was out in the political dumpster two years later. If there were a way for people to vote with their cable remotes, nobody would stay in office long enough to draw a paycheck.

The government hasn't worked in a long time. People are frustrated, and they'll take it out on anybody they can. But their choice is too limited, which is why nary a decade passes when the voters don't "destroy" one of the two major parties. But they go right back to them because there are only two games in town. And Perot doesn't count. He actually narrowed the choice. Ain't never been a revolution worth a damn that was started by a billionaire. If'n ole Ross don't like that, he can take it out 'hind the shed and hump it for all I care.

Newt rode high for a while, but then his fortunes shifted. On June 11, 1995, a white-bearded prophet walked upon the water and cast out a demon—along with his fishing line. He also cast a pall over atheists because after what happened that glorious Sunday morning, many of us concluded that there must be a God.

The setting was biblically idyllic: the wilderness. The main players were equally appropriate: a fisherman of peace—Tim Kipp, a forty-eight-year-old history teacher from Brattleboro,

Vermont, a false prophet—Newt Gingrich a fifty-one-year-old history reviser from Marietta, Georgia, and loads of scribes, as in the national or better yet, multi-national, press corps.

Kipp sets the scene, "At first we thought it was a funeral—all the lights, ten to fifteen cars and a big bus and then they stopped right next to us and I thought what the hell is going on here? And then Newty gets out and says, 'Hi, I'm Newt! I'm Newt Gingrich!' And then when I heard that, I just slooooowly turned and that's when it all started." It sure did. Tim caught four trout that day. He also had several thousand bites. Sound bites.

"Once the press corps realized I wasn't some country bumpkin out fishing and I wasn't going to be falling all over the speaker of the house and I was going to be on the attack . . . they just came forward. They were ignited by it. And then I let loose on him."

Let loose he did, greeting Gingrich with "Your politics are some of the meanest politics, I've ever heard. You make *Calvin Coolidge look like a liberal.*"

Kipp describes what followed. "He [Gingrich] was taken aback but then recomposed his cute little politician style. And said 'Good line.' Adding, 'Despite our political differences, good luck.'

"Then I wouldn't stop, I continued [to address the media as Gingrich beat a hasty retreat]. This guy is the most mean-spirited, vicious politician we've seen in a long time. The water we're fishing in will be destroyed by his policies. There will be *nothing* left when he is through.'"

Unfortunately there was enough left of Gingrich to attempt to spin his way out of the confrontation later with ersatz regal beneficence explaining, "I wanted you guys to get the photo-op." Obviously, Newt didn't estimate that the odds were well in his favor when he stopped to chat with two "sportsmen" in New Hampshire. No, he was just acting on an altruistic impulse to assist the media. "This guy can go back for the rest of his life and say, 'I stood up for what I believe in.' That's fine. That's what America is all about."

What Gingrich didn't know is there is nothing new about Tim Kipp's speaking his mind—even to a member of congress. His own congressman, Bernie Sanders—INDEPENDENT, VERMONT regularly seeks Kipp's input and insight. He serves as a Sanders campaign coordinator. He is also an important member of Vermont's very vibrant Progressive Coalition. I met Tim in 1990, when I was performing at fundraisers for Sanders. We crossed paths and have remained in sporadic contact since but had not been in touch for some time when I heard his articulate admonishments of Gingrich as I was checking CNN for baseball scores. At the time I said "that looks like . . . oh my God . . . it is TIM!!! NAILING GINGRICH!!! In his extremely audible TEACHER VOICE. What are the odds?? Gingrich hits the reverse lottery!!" I died laughing.

I regained my composure a few days later and called Tim. The twenty-two-year educator was bemused by the karmic irony but displeased with the treatment the press was giving him in the interviews. "They wanted to know, of course what happened, and I'm trying to weave in stuff on the Contract [on America], facts about the Contract—a $225 billion tax break—welfare for the rich, free enterprise for the rest of us . . . that stuff. It was really hard to get in. They were really uninterested in the motivations of why someone would be angry with this reactionary. They just wanted the *ha-ha* of making this guy's jaw drop for a few minutes."

Kipp took particular exception to the *New York Times* account of what has to be the greatest left-wing fishing story since Jesus was promoting socialism. He laughed. "They said I was wearing camouflage. I would never wear camouflage. I'm not in the Vermont Militia. Anyway why wear camouflage in the middle of the Androscoggin River? To fool the fish?"

His assessment of fellow educator Gingrich? "He takes terrible corporate history and conventional mainstream history and makes it even worse."

His own students seem to have a much higher opinion of Mr. Kipp. He was voted 1994–1995 Teacher of the Year at Brattleboro High School. This was prior to his evisceration of Gingrich. Considering what Gingrich's policies mean to public schools, Tim seems a shoo-in for Teacher of the Decade.

Kipp responded to Gingrich's attempt to damn him with faint praise. "I don't know when *he* got politically active, but the first time I was on a demonstration was 1966. I've been on picket lines, in demonstrations, and organizing since then. No, Newt, this isn't the first time I have spoken out about what I believe in. This is nothing new, it's just part of a lifestyle and political mindset. He made the assumption that this was my one and only shot at some kind of political statement, when in fact my whole life represents a progressive humanistic struggle. And I'm proud of that."

From that point on, Gingrich was never the same. By 1998 he was being held accountable for four years of political obscenity.

As the future former Speaker of the House's dreams of a thousand-year Republican Reich toppled about him, Newt greeted sunrise on the day after the 1998 election the same way he left us the previous evening: looking shifty and defeated in the network glare. He told commentators he was upset that African Americans had turned out in large numbers to vote 8–1 against his party. The Speaker came just short of bemoaning the upgrade blacks had received from three-fifths-of-a-man status after the Civil War that had led us to this sorry day.

He blamed the media's focus on the Clinton-Lewinsky affair for the failure of the American people to increase the Republican majority in the House of Representatives. Had Gingrich not been retreating into a comfortable cocoon of shock, even he would have felt just a bit of shame for attempting to dump such a fetid load of manure.

A several-million-dollar last-minute G O P T V splurge in thirty key congressional districts had consisted of nothing more than advertisements of the fact that Clinton had an affair. And this inane maneuver was forever etched with Gingrich's imprimatur. He could not escape it.

How even Gingrich could be so blind is hard to fathom. What possible need was there to advertise the fact that Bill Clinton had committed adultery? Who didn't know that? Had the Republicans forgotten that the previous August, Clinton gave a speech, aired worldwide, admitting this sordid behavior? Had it slipped their minds how our national water pressure dropped as we all ran in and showered after watching our president confess to such cheesy conduct? Americans made it clear that although we don't endorse the president's behavior, we discern a difference between lying about a sexual affair and, say, authorizing a break-in at a political opponent's headquarters. Had they missed that, too?

Ironically, had Gingrich not pressed his luck, the G O P might have held on to enough seats in the House to move quickly toward impeachment. Maybe the party would even have picked up enough votes in the Senate to guarantee Clinton's ouster. Instead, the Dems gained five seats in the House and held their own in the Senate.

So on Wednesday morning, as Gingrich lied to the media with much less verve than usual, the truth was simple. He had played a major role in reelecting a president who wasn't even on the ballot or eligible to run for another term.

After that, it was just a matter of time before his party's bloodlust, originally focused on Clinton, would be satiated by the ample flesh of Newt Gingrich. He had trained the House Republicans, and they learned their lessons well. We now know why Newt looked so uncomfortable on T V that first morning. It is hard to lean back and relax when your back is full of daggers.

What do you bet W's investigation into Halliburton's gas-price gouging in Iraq will identify the failure to open the Arctic National Wildlife Reserve to oil drilling as the real culprit?

Bush didn't visit Iraq so much as have a layover there.

It would be like you or me making a connection at O'Hare and then bragging about how we really got a chance to know Chicago.

"And here's a picture of me with the skycaps who are synonymous with the Windy City."

"Wow! Chicago is just full of duty-free shops and there are news kiosks everywhere!"

"Many of the older natives travel by golf cart."

eleven

The Hub of the Comedy Universe

I n the mid-1970s, I took my increased fluency in counter-cultural language and customs, traveled around the country, and began hustling standup comedy appearances. For a large portion of 1977 I imposed upon my pal Woody Abel in San Francisco. Woody and I had become friends during the year we spent together at the University of Miami in Coral Gables, Florida. (When asked what I studied at the U of M, I always replied "I took the one-year smuggling program.") In San Fran I got a chance to see a vibrant comedy scene early in its development. I regularly signed up for open-mike nights at places like the Holy City Zoo and got some stage time, but never enough. But I met and befriended real comics for the first time in my life. Foremost among them was A. Whitney Brown, already a big star in the Bay Area. He couldn't have been more supportive or magnanimous toward an unknown. In early 1978 I headed back east and managed to continue my patchwork career by convincing club owners to allow me to do five or ten minutes between sets by local rock acts in bars throughout the northeast. You really have to learn how to hit the stage running when your audience is a looming, drunken, stoned mob, with ears ringing from a cover of *Smoke on the Water* that somehow managed to miss the subtleties of Deep Purple's original anthem.

Worn from the travail of juggling a comedy career with home-lessness, I returned to Skaneateles although my family no longer lived there. Still, as long as I had many friends and an indigenous knowledge of area barns, back lots, and camps on the lake, home-town homelessness presented far fewer hardships than the itiner-ant brand I'd practiced around much of the country. I convinced my pal Lee "Skeeter" Crossley (on the Phil Crimmins-coached Skaneateles Yankees he was the pitcher and I was the catcher) to let me do a comedy show at his popular restaurant and bar, Under the Stone in the village. Skeeter at times allowed me to unfurl a sleeping bag in an unused portion of the basement of what had once been Skaneateles' grain mill. Unfortunately, the health department frowned on restaurant-flophouses so I was usually on my own, and it made for some chilly nights. It didn't take many such evenings to shiver any residual Republicanism from my bones. Needless to state, I'm always happy to appear at benefits for the homeless.

I couldn't do a new show alone every week (we had BIG repeat audiences), and so I roped Steve Leahy, the funniest bartender in town, into forming a comedy team with me. We'd both do a set of standup, some sketches, and a weekly news roundup, the Crimmins-Leahy Report. Steve was already a great comic when, after several months of helping me pack the joint on Wednesday nights, he decided to leave the show to study hotel management at Paul Smith's College. When Steve departed, I placed an ad for other comics in the Syracuse *New Times* and hit pay dirt. Wendell Wild, who later became something of a cult legend from one cassette of his I used to play on the way to gigs for other comics, was the first to check in. On the tape Wild took a number of currently ubiquitous terms and activities, like Frisbee-throwing, wine and cheese parties, going cross-country, putting a bandana on your dog and mixed and matched them to uproarious effect—putting a bandana on cheese, cross-country dog throwing, wine and Frisbee parties, and so on. The cumula-tive effect of his calm and relentless delivery combined with the sheer audacity it took to commit to such an unorthodox piece and stick to it for a seeming on-stage eternity made Wild a thinking comic's thinking comic. Wendell, quintessentially too hip for the room, eventually became a social worker in Buffalo, where he has quietly helped thousands of people over the years. He 's also an outstanding freelance writer. Wendell and his wife, Gail Nicholson, a writer and arts activist, remain among my dearest friends. Much of what I do or say in public has been improved by Wendell's astute eye and munificent suggestions.

The next call was from two high-school kids: Bob Goldthwait and Tom Kenny, both were destined for serious show biz glory. They were unbelievably funny from their first appearance, and neither has let up since. Goldthwait went on to do recordings, movies, TV specials and series. Tom has done all sorts of stuff as an actor and standup, including adding even more genius to HBO's *Mr. Show* than David Cross (a latter-day Boston alum and friend) and Bob Odenkirk already brought to it. If you have kids or adults with a sense of humor, you may also know Tom as Spongebob Squarepants, the cartoon star.

My father, who had been in the VA hospital in Washington, DC, was moved to the facility in Martinsburg, West Virginia. He was quite ill and so I left my duties as producer and performer to hitchhike down to see him. After several days he got better, and so I stuck out my thumb and headed north, figuring I'd go to New York to try to find some stage time. Instead, the second person to pick me up was going to Boston. I figured "what the heck" and took the ride. I knew a woman there, and besides, the Red Sox were there, and so it was a Big Leagues town.

Things didn't go so great with my woman friend; within a few days it was Memorial Day weekend and I was on the street. I found a listing in the Boston *Globe* for a show produced by the Comedy Connection at a club called the Springfield Street Saloon in Inman Square in Cambridge. Having done comedy in other cities, I figured my only chance of wangling a guest set would be to get there in the afternoon and stake a claim. I arrived at the club at about 2:30, all my worldly belongings in hand. The place was locked and a sign indicated that it would not open for a few more hours.

I walked back into Inman Square and started considering how to hitch out of Boston. As I meandered unsurely up the street I heard music emanating from a place called the InnSquare Men's Bar/ Ladies Invited. I walked in, baggage in hand, trying not to look too conspicuously homeless.

A red-haired man behind the bar was not easily fooled. He said, "What can I get you after I hide that suitcase so everyone doesn't notice your pitiful condition?" And then he smiled. That was the first time I ever met Chris Bracken. He had played in Country Granola, a band from Ithaca that I saw perform at Under the Stone. In the next few hours Bracken let me pay for exactly zero beers as we chatted like we were something we would eventually become—old friends. I disclosed the grim nature of my circumstances and explained how I was considering leaving town. He encouraged me to stay around and go over to do the show. When his shift ended, he admonished the night staff to "Take care of my friend, Barry. Whatever he wants."

I spent another half-hour with my old acquaintance Nurse Beer and headed back to the Springfield Street Saloon. I really liked the room; it was jammed with 125 fans on a three-day-weekend Sunday night. The guys who ran the show told me two things I needed to know. First, they said, Boston would never be a weekend comedy town. And second, they said that they liked my act, which was why they were paying me all of $8. They admonished me not to disclose their largesse to the other. That was all I needed to hear: with these Boy Scouts running things, Boston was ripe for a new comedy venue.

I decided to stay in town, but it wasn't easy. I found one of the last vacant forested areas in Cambridge and made a small campsite for myself. Many nights I just slept near a place called Labor Pool in the South End, where I jockeyed for position with a collection of down-and-out people hoping to get temp work for the day. During this period I worked as a fish packer, ship painter, and potato-chip shipper, among many other really bad jobs. Every fourth or fifth day I'd take my collected earnings and rent a room at the YMCA at Northeastern. This meant a few days of TV, private bath, clean linens, and a bed. I'd hit used bookstores and grab Twain, Hunter Thompson, Kurt Vonnegut, and Garry Trudeau's *Doonesbury* collections as well as the local alternative papers, the *Boston Phoenix* and the *Real Paper*. Between my desperate circumstances and the underground reading material, my subversion was nearly complete.

At about this time the Springfield Street Saloon was sold to a man named Shune Lee. Shune was a classic character with a rough story. As a small child his family had left him behind when they escaped Mainland China. The thinking was that they would be less suspicious as they made for the border because no one would expect them to leave a son behind. A few years later, "an old lady" carried Shune to freedom. "I not even know her name!"

Shune and I hit it off famously. He was still booking a lot of the bands that had played at the club prior to his ownership, but they weren't drawing well and cost a lot of money. I asked how the comedy nights were, and he said, "Great. Good crowd, many come for dinner and they drink. Plus it cost no money, Comedy Connection just get door."

I'm not demeaning Shune's speech, just quoting how he spoke. His English was far ahead of my Chinese. He kept the club's Western decor but changed the menu to Chinese and the name to the Ding Ho. I found a room in Inman Square and found a job painting condos right around the corner. Things were looking up.

I frequented the Ding and helped Shune Lee by running errands and dealing with an unruly patron or two. One night the bouncer disappeared,—just split during his shift. I took over for the rest of the evening. The next time I came to the club, Shune offered me the bouncing job.

So I stood outside the bar and greeted customers. When people would ask if the band was good, I would say, "I work here; the boss is standing right behind me. No, the band sucks; I think you should go next door." The people would laugh, pay their $3, and enter. Shune was impressed. "That was good. Very good job."

The first night Shune put me in charge of paying the band, which he hated doing. Within a few days I was booking the club. Within two months the Springfield Street Saloon had become the Ding Ho, Home of Constant Comedy. The Ding honored all its musical commitments, so for the first few weeks we double-billed music and comedy. But soon it became Greater Boston's first full-time comedy club. These days in comedy joints, you don't see the headliner until the audience has suffered through two often lowest-common-denominator acts. Then halfway into the headliner's act, just when the audience is showing signs of healing, the wait staff passes out the checks and sticker shock sets in.

We did it better at the Ding. The star hosted the show. If there was no host, we went tag team and had one comic introduce the next, the rookies brought on by the vets. It was topnotch from the start of each performance because vets enliven audiences better than novices.

We began by using Lenny Clarke, Don Gavin, Chance Langton, Teddy Bergeron, Mike Donovan, and Mike McDonald as hosts. Langton booked and produced his own shows on Saturdays and did a fabulous job. I produced the rest of the nights.

Extraordinary acts and top-shelf hosts made for great shows. Bill Campbell; Jay Charbonneau; Ken Ober; Joe Alaskey, a phenomenal impressionist who eventually moved to Los Angeles and replaced none other than Mel Blanc as Bugs Bunny and the rest of the Loony Tunesters; Paula Poundstone; Steven Wright; Bob (LaMotte) and Ron (Lynch); Lauren Dombrowski; John Ten-Eyck; Barry Niekrug; Bob Lazurus; George MacDonald; Warren MacDonald; Jack Gallagher; Bobby Gaylor; Jim Morris, whose scarily perfect channeling of Ronald Reagan provided some of the best political moments at the Ding; Dave Barbuto; Bob Siebel; and the late Chris Collins are just the names that I can summon without freebasing ginkgo biloba.

It didn't take a month for the Ding shows to start selling out. Lenny Clarke's Wednesday open-mike night was impossible to get into even a half-hour before he took the stage; he was a Cambridge boy who led his entire hometown through the Ding's doors and then knocked their socks off with his raw and explosive comedy. When I finally left the production end of things at the Ding, I turned my duties over to his brother Mike Clarke, who is still a very successful comedy producer and manager.

Paula Poundstone was just a teenager when she auditioned before several veteran performers at the Comedy Connection. Mike McDonald recalls, "Within ninety seconds she knew that she hadn't prepared the proper material and rather than panic she calmly told us, 'This isn't working. I need twenty minutes.' And then twenty minutes later she came back and *killed* with new material she had improvised under inordinate pressure. I'll be damned if I can remember a line she said, but from that moment on she was a welcome member of the comedy community." She was an original member of the Ding's first team.

It was an elite company. You had to hit the stage running when you followed the likes of:

Bill Campbell discussing the life and death vicissitudes of driving in the Hub. "A yellow light means *get your ass moving*! And it's OK to go through a red light if it *just* turned. Only in Boston do you accidentally run a red light and say, 'Oh my god, I just ran a red light!' then look in your rearview mirror and see six *more* people run the same light."

Teddy Bergeron depicting a spoilsport at a live production of *Peter Pan*. "SHE'S ON A WIRE! THERE'S NO SANTA CLAUS AND SHE'S ON A WIRE!"

Don Gavin, dissecting the comic section: "I've read *Mutt and Jeff* every day for twenty-three years, and they *still* haven't had one good day." Gavin was the most calm and collected of the Boston acts. The most I could ever consume before a show was a beer or two, Gav could walk on the stage just as he finished eating lasagna and calmly go about the business of destroying an audience.

Mike Donovan was arguably the most gifted of all the acts. He was a polished pro from the first time I saw him work in 1979. He could do impressions and sound effects that perfectly illustrated his already topnotch material. And he was so hilarious. In a classic piece Mike sent up the huffy-puffy idiocy of television's cheesy double entendres, perfectly replicating the music, noises, and second-rate stars of a then-popular game show. "Put me on the Match Game and I'd teach them a lesson in honesty," and then, perfectly replicating Gene Rayburn: *"Mary said to Bob, 'Show me your Blank . . .'* Mike?"

"I'm gonna have to go with 'cock,' Gene."

Donovan's method for obtaining the correct time? "Rather than call that cold, heartless recording I just dial any old number at random."

Brrringgg! Brrringgg!

Very cobwebbed voice "Uhhh, hello?"

"Yes, can you tell me the time, please?"

"Well Jesus Christ, it's nearly four o'clock in the morning."

"Thank you!" Click!

Steven Wright was a genius from the start. Deadpan, hilarious, and artistically abstract, he arrived with the distilled essence of humor in tow, offering, "I have a map of the United States. It's actual size. I spent the summer folding it." Or "I met the man who invented Cliff Notes. I asked, 'How did you get started?' He said, 'Well, to make a long story short . . .'" And the all-time classic: "Two babies are born on the same day in the same hospital. Eighty years later by sheer coincidence, they end up dying in hospital beds next to each other. One turns to the other and says, 'Sooo . . . what did you think?'"

Steve Sweeney, the Character King of Boston, knew and replicated his hometown like no one else could. In rapid-fire talk he'd introduce, among numerous others. John McGinty, the wino philosopher, "I stink, therefore I am." Master Sergeant Hugh Delaney, ever vigilantly warning us about the looming threat of "the ca-ca communists" and a local woman making singles-bar conversation with a man who offers, "Hello, I am Rudy. I am from India."

"India?" she'd query in the most hideous Bahstan eeyaksent you ever heard, "You know a kid named Kevin O'Malley?"

Brian Kiley, the most relentlessly decent person you'll ever meet in comedy, was a brilliant joke writer from the jump. He worried about his father's cotton allergy. "He has pills he can take—but he can't get them out of the bottle."

Kenny Rogerson, amid a stream-of-consciousness indictment of, of all things, bulbs (they are always there when there's trouble, on police cars, ambulances and so on) would start talking about electric Christmas displays and rant. "There were no *bulbs* in the manger! One wise man never said to another, 'Hey flick on the light, I can't see the kid. Ah jeeze, I've been kneeling over a *goat* for half an hour.'"

Kenny was also fond of telling about the time he was arrested for hitting . . . a lake. "These damn foreign cars crap out at a couple of fathoms, officer."

"Have you been drinking, Mr. Rogerson?"

"How many *sober people* do you know that hit *lakes*?"

:::

Some things had to be seen to be truly appreciated, like Lauren Dombrowski killing on stage doing a Fred Flintstone outtake on a blooper show—"Aww Fuck, sorry Wilma. Can I try that again?"—as her identical twin sister, Lynn (a civilian but also very funny), sat roaring in the audience.

Chance Langton ignited Ding crowds with wry asides: "On the way here tonight I heard that Gloria Gaynor song, "I Will Survive." Hey, whatever happened to her?"

Kevin Meaney was such a naturally charismatic performer that he could manipulate one piece of relatively flimsy material until everyone was asphyxiated from laughter. He'd take the days of the week and sing them, and just when people thought it was finally over, he switched to the months of the year. Upon reaching December, he burst into the numbers. "1, 2, 3, 4, 5, 6, 7, 8, 9, 10, 11, 12. I said 13, 14, 15, 16, 17, 18 19, 20 . . ." Had enough? Ding crowds never did.

Young acts who worked the Ding's open-mike nights before graduating to paid gigs included Tom Gilmore, Dana Gould, Jonathan Groff, Joe Yannety, Denis Leary, Bill Braudis, Jim DeCroteau, Dan Margarita, Mike Bent, Linda Smith, Johnny Pizzi, and Jimmy Tingle. Tingle became the day bartender at the Ding and added to the genuine Cambridge character of the club. Eventually he would succeed Lenny as the open-mike host. After that, succeeding became one of Jimmy's habits. Tingle went on to become a commentator on *60 Minutes II* and now has his own theater in Somerville.

Bobcat Goldthwait used to open his sets by announcing, "My mother had a baby and its head popped off!" And then he'd move on to the outrageous stuff. He didn't stay in Boston long, instead opting for San Francisco, where he quickly overwhelmed the scene out there.

In October of 1999 Jimmy Tingle organized a reunion of the Ding Ho alumni to mark the twentieth anniversary of the founding of the club. An electrified sell-out crowd witnessed a spectacular night at the Somerville Theater. A few dozen of the greatest acts—ever—got up and entertained and reminisced for over three hours. The audience roared appreciation for every minute of the show. I was singled out for excessive and effusive praise for my role at the Ding and beyond. I was also the beneficiary of the night because I had been ill and, being an American artist, had no health insurance. I was deeply touched by the generosity and love shown by my old, dear and extremely talented friends.

Of course several of them used the occasion to recall why I'll never have to worry about impending sainthood.

One of my favorites came when Bobcat interrupted his rollicking to reflect, "There's another Barry that hasn't been addressed too much this evening. That would be the Barry that maybe even Barry doesn't remember so well.

"One night in the mid-1980s I got a call at 3 AM at my house. I pick up the phone and I hear, 'Uhh, Goldthwait, you SUCK!'
    "I go, 'Hello? Who is this?'
    "It's me, Crimmins. You suck!'
    "And I say, 'Well what did I do wrong, Barry?'
    "And he says, "Nothing! I'm drunk and I wanted to call a movie star and tell him he sucks."

It *had* slipped my mind, but when Goldy told the story, it brought it all back to me. Ah, memories.

Along the way we gathered Goldthwait from Syracuse, Meaney, Mike Moto, and Fran and Jan (the Solomita Brothers) from San Francisco, Rogerson and Paul Kozlowski (from Chicago), and Bob Nickman and Phil Van Tee (from Cleveland). All became Ding stalwarts, keeping patrons in stitches until the bar closed.

Not that the bar closed very often—except to the general public. The Ding stretched its liquor-license luck on a nightly basis. Nearly as much alcohol was consumed after hours as during the shows. The restaurant was in the back and windowless. So before it got too late, we'd move the party out there and, in the immortal words of that ringleader of ringleaders, Don Gavin, "hurt ourselves."

At least our late nights put the dining room to positive use. As Sweeney used to say, "Ding Ho in Chinese means bad food."

Eventually the restaurant became the auxiliary showroom. You'd do a set in the front room, take a breath, and walk out back and do the next. By evening's end half the comics in town had found their way to the Ding. There were some mighty parties—the biggest on the first anniversary of the Constant Comedy venue. Everyone performed at a gala show—and then the frivolity really began. At 8 AM on Saturday, October 4, 1980, when it was again a legal hour to have the bar open, I counted more than fifty people coming back through the doors into the main room. Most didn't stay much past 11 AM. After all, we had shows to do that night.

One evening Lenny and I had been practicing our drinking until the microscopic hours of the morning. We summoned our good friend and personal Green Cab driver Edward "Trigger" Burke to take us in search of breakfast. Lenny said that he knew just the place, and a few minutes later we pulled up in a side street just outside of Harvard Square. He ordered me out of the cab, and I followed him up the walk of one of the posh homes. There wasn't a light on in the place. "Where the hell are we?" I asked.

Lenny said, "We're at someone's home who would just loooove cooking us some breakfast." And with that he began pounding on the door and yelling, "Get up! We want some eggs!" Sure enough, lights came on and after a commotion, two snarling dogs, German shepherds I think, came tearing toward the door.

With that, Lenny turned tail and sprinted back to the cab. I matched him stride for stride and dove in just as Ed stood on the pedal so hard that both our doors closed from the resulting massive rout of inertia. Lenny was howling with laughter by this time and finally composed himself enough to say, "Jesus Christ, you'd think fucking *Julia Child* would enjoy doing a little cooking."

When we weren't terrorizing elderly P B S icons, we worked very hard to keep up with our brilliant peers at a time when Boston and American comedy scenes were experiencing breakout success. The secret of the Ding was that it was of, by, and for comics. The club treated all its acts like stars. Comics didn't pay for drinks—ever. They could put anyone they liked on the guest list. If a comic's family came in, we wined and dined them (at least by Ding Ho standards), gushing about their talented and wonderful loved one. Perhaps the most important thing the Ding did for young comics was to make their show-business aspirations seem legitimate to parents and family.

We had almost no money for advertising, even after constant sellouts, because Shune Lee's business skills and my comics-drink-free policy pushed the Ding to the brink of fiscal calamity. Fortunately, D. J. Hanard (now legally changed to "Hazzard"), a local comic and art student I'd engaged to do the Constant Comedy logo, made memorable signs and fliers. D. J. kept the Ding running with his artistic and technical expertise, and then he'd walk out on the stage and devastate the audience. Early on, D. J. and I attached ourselves to W C A S radio in Central Square—a gem of a low-power, low-budget community station specializing in folk-rock, country-mawk, and populist Cantabrigian public-affairs shows—and began the Constant Comedy radio program. We offended everyone from Catholics (we did a "rush hour for Catholics" report on Sunday mornings from our Catholic Copter) to Iranians (this was hostage-crisis time; Lenny came up with Iranian Round-up Day.) Some of my friends on the left took these and other send-ups literally, and soon we were skewering them by representing them on the air with what Sweeney labeled The Cambridge Coalition Against Humor. His dozens of remarkable characters provided major ballast for the show. Martin Olson, the Ding's legendary piano player, now a very hot scribe in Los Angeles, was also a huge contributor to the radio effort as both a writer and a performer. Some weeks our program was hilarious, some weeks it sounded like a bunch of guys who had kept partying long after the midnight show. But we gave them a comedy once a week, and each time WCAS ran a promo for the show, it included a kicker about the Ding.

Steven Wright was the first Ding comic to hit it big. Peter Lassally, the executive producer from the Tonight Show, came to the club to look at Boston talent, and a few weeks later Steven got the call. Johnny Carson loved him; America loved him. Carson asked him back. Four days after his first appearance Steven came back and killed on the Tonight Show—again.

Since Steven busted the wedge and became a Grammy-nominated, Oscar-winning international comedy star, almost everyone who ever performed at the Ding has gone on to bigger things. If you watch television or movies, you can't go long without seeing Ding Ho alums on the screen or in the credits. Lenny stars in the ABC sitcom *It's all Relative*, Sweeney hosts Boston's highest-rated morning radio show on WZLX-FM. Goldthwait has reached Show Biz Nirvana—he directs. Lauren Dombrowski is the executive producer of *Mad tv*. After taking some lumps, my old friend Paula Poundstone is back on stage and more brilliant than ever. George MacDonald wrote and starred in a hit play about the missing South Boston gangster Whitey Bulger. Brian Kiley is Conan O'Brien's senior staff writer. Martin Olson just sold a screenplay to a major studio. Don Gavin recently killed on Letterman. D.J. just finished a standout run in a standup series on Comedy Central, Bob Nickman is an exec producer on the sitcom *The World According to Jim*, Mike Donovan and Mike

McDonald are still performing in Boston when they aren't off taping a TV show somewhere or gigging in some far-flung locale. Jack Gallagher is touring with his smash one-man show *Waiting for Declan*. And word has it that Kevin Meaney is heading for Broadway; they'd better have a pretty big stage.

As best I can determine, the cause of death at the Ding was unpaid taxes resulting from Shune's gambling losses playing mah-jongg in Chinatown. The last time I ever saw Shune Lee was at the Ding Ho on a Saturday night when we sold out four shows. A few days later, when I dropped by the club to pick up a notebook, there were plywood sheets hammered over the doors.

Fortunately the Boston comedy scene had grown by then. I had moved across town and started Stitches in the front room of the Paradise, with the help of local impresarios Don Law and Patrick Lyons. The Comedy Connection was thriving, Nick's Comedy Stop was doing big business, Chance Langton got things hopping at a club called Play It Again Sam's. There were regular well-paying gigs throughout New England, and Boston comics were welcome nationwide. The Ding had failed, but the Ding had paved the way. It proved that good comics, treated well in a good room, could find an audience almost every night of the year. It proved that comedy was here to stay. Most important, it proved that Boston was the home of some of the best comedic talent—and some of the worst Chinese food—in the world.

President George W. Bush has named war criminal emeritus Henry Kissinger to head the "independent" commission to investigate the 9/11/01 attacks. Since neither Pol Pot nor Augusto Pinochet were available, Kissinger was the obvious choice.

What is Kissinger going to do? Assign style points for carnage? "Vell, I vood haff decapitated a few more people but zat izz yust a madder ov perzonal preverence. On balance, vor a virst evfort, zay did some nize vork."

Who better to investigate and bring light to the 9/11 massacres than a man who once tried to keep *the carpet bombing of entire nation* secret?

Henry Kissinger now says he's certain Saddam has chemical weapons. Apparently he dug through the Kissinger & Associates files and found a receipt.

twelve

Never Shake Hands
with a War Criminal

Recently the debate over whether or not Henry Kissinger is a war criminal has become a hot topic. Kissinger himself seems convinced that he is what lawyers call actionable. He has ceased a lifetime of globetrotting out of fear that a process server might hand him an International Criminal Court summons instead of the diplomatic pouch full of Krugerrands he was expecting. The timing for this push for accountability couldn't be worse. With George W. Bush in power, Kissinger could be profiteering with caprice. Now he must commit his acts of multinational skullduggery through intermediaries. Since the man who invented the idea of secret carpet bombing trained his operatives, he knows they can't be trusted.

I'll give Kissinger credit for one thing; he showed great restraint when he didn't contest Pol Pot's will a few years ago. Nobody could have argued that Henry wasn't deserving of at least the mineral rights to the Killing Fields.

I wouldn't make a good member of Kissinger's ICC jury. For one thing, I long ago decided on his guilt or innocence. And although I could technically say I never formally met the man, we do have a small bit of shared history. I'd like to think our moment in time comes back to Henry every now and then—in nightmares.

It was the Friday before the 1988 Michigan Primary. I was at CNN's New York studios to do a talk show to discuss the presidential race. I was chatting with Norma Quarles, a CNN anchor, in the Green Room. We were maybe fifty stories up in a New

York City office building. She was sitting on a couch; I was pacing in front of her on the other side of a coffee table, nervously preparing to go on the air. She was very nice and laughed at much of what I had to say. Suddenly she looked right past me and began sucking up to someone at a clip that was fantastic even for a corporate news anchor.

She was dropping names something furious, stating, "Oh hello, Doctor! We were at so-and-so's with you and such and such from so on and so forth."

I turned to look at the person who had just entered the room. Quarles faded into the background as rage possessed me. By the door was someone I didn't at first recognize but I immediately felt H A T R E D toward. Inside my head I began to criticize myself for having such instantly vile feelings until I realized, "Wait a minute, *that's Henry Kissinger!* Oh, O K." And then I patted myself on the soul for being a good watchdog.

While this realization was taking place, I bootlegged around the entire perimeter of the room so as to not walk directly toward the black hole of evil by the door. I wanted and was getting O U T.

Kissinger was already warming up to the situation, but he had missed something. While responding to Quarles, he had not assessed me, at least not properly. As I got to the doorway, Henry was just clear of it, inside just to its right, as he faced the room. I was coming from (appropriately enough) his left. He turned to face me, apparently having guessed that I was scurrying away because I didn't deem myself worthy to be in his presence. He was standing there, sort of bubbling evil, making those Kissinger idling sounds, like a satanic water cooler. ("Bulaaaahh, bulaaaah" or something like that. It's hard to spell in demon.) To demonstrate his magnanimity, either to impress Quarles or because he badly misjudged me and figured I was deferentially bailing out, he gave me a chance to stay and lurk in humble worship.

He extended his claw and said, "Ehhhhhelloo, I em Enree Kizzzengerrrr."

I looked him right in the eye and his confidence instantly deteriorated to panic. In a nanosecond he understood that he was a small and frail older man in the presence of a relatively young man, large enough to pick him up and crash him through the windows across the room to sure death on the street.

Lucky for Kissinger I don't think like him. I'm not a killer. All I did was scowl and growl. "Urrgggghhhhhhh."

Our eye contact spoke volumes. For just a few seconds this man, to whom death and agony were side dishes, was put into a fair confrontation. There was no security to protect him and his escape route was cut off. I was between him and his normal phalanx of defense. As I left, his hand was still in midair, the only part of him unshaken. He looked like a one-armed zombie. I didn't fully understand all that transpired in that instant until a minute later, when I was pacing in the hall outside the room, by then badly frazzled. Kissinger is so sinister, so guilty that I needed nothing more than my eyes to let him know that there were people like me in the world who saw his evil and would not acquiesce to it, even for a few clumsy moments in a TV studio waiting room.

Kissinger or Quarles must have gotten to a phone. Security and PR types materialized and zoomed past me as they headed for the Green Room. No one did or said anything to me as I loomed in the hall, a smart and safe distance away. They just ringed Kissinger and escorted him into another area. Within a few moments I was back in the Green Room. Ms. Quarles was still on the couch.

As I leaned over to retrieve my notebook from the coffee table, she asked, "Why didn't you shake hands with Dr. Kissinger?"

"Because I have a strict policy of never shaking hands with war criminals," says I.

"Oh, *that's* right. I'd forgotten," said Norma Quarles. Maybe it was precise truth, maybe she was humoring a lunatic, maybe she was simply showing grudging respect for anyone who was capable of standing up to evil, if only by walking away from it.

Many times in life we think of what we should have said after a confrontation. This was not the case when I crossed paths with Henry Kissinger.

I read that one freedom-loving NRA supporter asked why guns are any different from kitchen knives or hammers. He reasoned that both could be used as murder weapons, just like a gun. That's a good point. I'd hate to count all of the random people killed each year, in public, by mass murderers using high-powered kitchen knives and hammers.

OK, we need a complete list of all Olympic hammer throwers in the capital area.

Who can forget that those kids from Columbine and the Veg-A-Matic they used in their killing spree?

America speaks with one voice. Unfortunately it emanates from its ass.

thirteen

Incident on Sixth Avenue

I was about a block and a half from my meeting at 30 Rockefeller Plaza in Manhattan on the first genuinely chilly day of autumn. I was three steps past him before I found the courage to walk back. I needed every inch of the extra distance to muster up the intestinal fortitude necessary to confront the most disturbing image I had seen in person for a very long time: an extremely thin child slumped and shivering against the base of a skyscraper. He was shoeless and naked except for the plastic trash bag he had fashioned into a toga.

I approached him slowly, so as not to startle him and because there was no guessing how he would respond to any human contact that exceeded dropping a coin in the filthy paper cup he clutched.

He appeared to be near death yet maintained dignity with eyes that betrayed a brave and logical decision. If this world could so abandon him, he would be glad to return the favor. He seemed to say, "You can do no more to me, I can have no less, I am none too fond or attached to this awful place, I mean no one any injury, that I am an insult to your eyes is a coincidence that was not provoked by any malice on my part."

Just as I entered the tiny space, that along with the garbage bag and cup, consisted of all that was his, a braver soul who did not need extra steps to assess the situation came over and said, "It's all right, I'm a Christian, do you have a family? Do you have a shelter?"

The boy's eyes began to focus on planet earth again just as this "Christian" did something that would have made Jesus Christ very proud—he took off his coat and said, "Jesus loves you and wants you to have this coat."

The child recoiled fearfully at the Samaritan's physical extension of the jacket toward him, terrified at the thought of anyone's touch. But the man's kindness and decency overwhelmed the child's fears after he reassured him, "I'm a Christian. Jesus loves you. I love you. It's OK, I'm giving you this because you should be warm." Convinced, the child permitted the garment to be wrapped about him.

Just then a security guard from the building approached—not to drive the child off but to say, "You are sick, son, and you need help. It's on the way. I've called an ambulance." Out of nowhere an EMT materialized with a blanket and said, " Are you all right son? Are you sick?"

The boy looked around, assessing the EMT, the coatless Samaritan, the security guard, and me. He made a leap of faith and broke his silence with a beautiful voice that said apologetically, "I think I have a cold." The EMT assured him, "We'll take care of that, we're going to bring you somewhere warm where they'll take care of you. All right?"

The boy nodded guarded approval, and seconds later was whisked away in an ambulance, out of sight but engraved in our souls forever.

Outside of putting some money in his cup and attempting to provide a kind and protective presence, I did or said nothing of significance during the six or seven minutes it took the drama to unfold.

As the Samaritan and I headed back up the sidewalk, I extended my hand to him and praised him for his kindness, compassion, and generosity. He once again stressed, "I'm a Christian. Sometimes talk isn't enough, sometimes you have to take action."

People like this man could give Christianity a good name.

With that he rounded the corner, without what may have been his only jacket, leaving me behind humbled and more determined to do whatever it takes to make this world a place where children are nurtured, protected, and safe, rather than discarded like rubbish in a trash bag.

Heartwarming news from AOL: Jan Brandt, the vermin behind those AOL discs that are mailed by the gross to every man, woman, and child in North America, has been fired. Let's hope they sent him three dozen copies of his pink slip.

And then, when he goes out shopping, he runs into a big display of his dismissal notices.

Brandt will take a new job distributing Chinese takeout menus in New York City.

fourteen

Broken Heartland

"So every human, and every place, is equal after all."
—Will Rogers

Where is the heartland? Geographically, it's the area defined by the central time zone. Metaphorically, it's a much broader place, a euphemism for Everywhere, USA. Last week, when terror tore the heart from the heartland, the first words on almost everyone's lips were, "Oklahoma City! Is nowhere safe?"

I have traveled for years in the heartland and found it full of redemptive encounters with good, honest, sincere, and surprisingly progressive people. But there is plenty to fear as well.

Contrary to popular belief, the heartland is not such a good neighborhood. It is a heavily armed camp. It is full of religious fundamentalists, paramilitarists, white supremacists, anti-Semites, skinheads, survivalists, neo-Nazis, and various other fringe wackos disturbed about plots that couldn't be devised by Kurt Vonnegut with a headful of bad acid. They are paranoid, weapons wealthy, filled beyond capacity with hatred, and capable of distilling all these "attributes" into something they call patriotism.

They worship at the altar of violence and impugn the common decency of anyone who questions their "religious freedom." They hide in our nation's vastness and mix with millions of average, innocent, harmless people. The innocents are aptly summed up as "the great dull bulk of the nation" by son of the heartland, Samuel Clemens.

Last Friday, when domestic paramilitarists became the prime suspects in the bombing, many people began to notice that

Oklahoma City is right between David Koresh and David Duke on the map.

You haven't heard the wind howl until you've listened to the screech it makes after blowing through four or five states unabated by things like trees or hills. It's eerie and lonely in the heartland. So when the people are friendly (as is usually the case), they seem friendlier. And when they're not, the desolation is amplified. At the end of vast expanses of flat emptiness a town will emerge. A teeny little outpost in the middle of great plains.

Minding my own business one morning in a diner in such a hamlet, I was assailed by a local for reading that dangerous leftist publication, USA Today. "How can you read that liberal crap?"

"I enjoy the Trotskyite sports writers," I replied, mostly because it was the smarmiest thing I could think of that I knew would not sink in. A more truthful rejoinder would have been this: "I only had it with me to avoid making eye contact with you."

I have always feared the Midwest more than the Middle East. That may be because I have never attempted to perform political satire in the Middle East. But playing the Midwest can be like having the Jihad and the Mossad sitting at adjacent tables.

There's irony in retracing alleged bomber Timothy McVeigh's steps through the heartland in the days leading to the bombing. Nowhere is the irony crueler than in the realization that the Gulf War veteran spent four nights at the Dreamland Motel in Junction City, Kansas—in the Desert Storm Room.

We have been warned for some time of the dangers of violent extremists within our borders. It is time for all of us to do whatever we can to thwart them. How can we do this? Well, what seems to threaten them the most is two words: One World, the simple concept that all of the earth's residents are in this together, that there is more to unite us than divide us. Promote the idea, talk it up. Call right-wing radio hosts and advocate One Worldism. Be sure to be very courteous and up about it. Apoplexy could well supplant apocalypse as today's topic.

In a fortuitous twist of fate no one has done more to promote the concept of One World than the despicable bomber(s) of the Alfred P. Murrah Federal Building. Because now that the twisted wreckage and unbelievable carnage have arrived on U.S. shores, Americans may finally face the truth: that such horror should visit no land. Residents of Iraq, Nicaragua, Panama, Libya, Grenada, Vietnam, or Cambodia know only too well what such visitations can mean. This time terror came to our own soil in a Ryder truck; too often it is flown in on the wings of a B-52.

An awful lot of conscience has come to us from Oklahoma. Woody Guthrie, Will Rogers, Steinbeck's Joad family, all rose from the Oklahoma prairie. Each reached into our hearts and made us feel a bond with the humanity and value of every American. If this latest cloud of Oklahoma dust clears and inspires that same respect for the lives of all the world's people, then we will have taken the very best of lessons from the very worst of teachers.

Philip Morris plans to change its name to the Altria Group. When asked if it bothered the corporation that "Altria" sounds a bit like "Al Qaida," a corporate spokesperson said, "What have they killed, a few thousand people? Get serious! Any association with those pikers improves our image."

An Al Qaida spokesman said, "Admittedly we suck, but unless Philip Morris changes its mind, we will have no choice but to slap them with a defamation of character suit."

American dissidents are finally being heard by their government. Who says wiretaps are such a bad thing?

fifteen

How Low Can We Go?

I n 1996 voters bestowed on Bill Clinton the honor of becoming the last sitting president to have won an election. But the fixation on his sex life reached the point where Al Gore nearly became what the American people voted for him to be a year or two early. By the spring of 1998 crotch fever had reached epic proportions.

In the early 1970s many comedians limited themselves almost exclusively to graphic sexual material. Not me. I shunned explicit sex talk for something with a much higher concentration of obscenity: hard-core politics.

So while others shocked and delighted audiences with the ins and outs of the human crotch, the only dick jokes I did involved a man named Nixon. With Nixon, assuming the worst was just an efficient use of one's time. He was guilty of nearly *everything*—war crimes, constitutional crimes, crimes of paranoia, hubris, judgment: you name it, Nixon did it. But there was one area of Tricky Dick's conduct that no one ever questioned—his sex life. If there was one immutable truth about Richard Nixon, it was this: nobody would ever *even consider* blowing the man.

My, how times have changed. Nowadays the only thing anyone seems to contemplate is the veracity of people who (reputedly) either fellated or refused to fellate Bill Clinton. Pretty cheesy, but things could be worse. Henry Kissinger could still be secretary of state.

Gennifer Flowers, Paula Jones, Kathleen Willey, and Monica Lewinsky are the four women who head up this story. Apparently

Clinton has admitted to cross-pollinating Flowers, who has parlayed her assignation with the then-governor of Arkansas into a semilucrative career as *Penthouse* model, third-rate nightclub warbler, and professional-wrestling ring girl. Of the four women, she has done the best. By far.

Then there is Paula Jones, who after several years in court was finally sent away with this information: "If you said no and he didn't persist, you have no case." Jones will eventually concentrate all of her energy on her true calling—her work as a punch line.

Then there was Kathleen Willey; she has offered the media various versions of an alleged sexual proposition made to her by the prez. She failed to hook the tabloids or book publishers, but she managed to sell the venerable *60 Minutes* on her tale of involvement with a presidential erection. Before *60 Minutes* viewers could flip over to *The Simpsons*, a White House spin squad had leaked Willey's own propositions to checkbook journalists, as well as the fan letters she wrote Clinton *after* the alleged encounter. Kathleen has faded fast; *60 Minutes* is still on the air.

Still jostling about the Ship of State is the loosest cannon of them all, Monica Lewinsky. When she first hit the news, it looked very bad for old Bill if the charges were true. Talk about a relationship power imbalance: on the one side you had a former intern, and on the other you had the chief executive of the United States of America. Impeachment talk was everywhere.

How could Clinton do this? I have my theories.

Having grown up fatherless, he has problems with self-esteem. He craves external approval. Which is why he loves campaigning and, especially, winning. But elections come only every few years; what to do between campaigns? How can he be sure others care for him? Through sex, that's how. The sad truth is that the president of the United States still can't believe women will actually touch him . . . you know, *down there*. Since he has found some women who will help relieve the pressures of power, he is driven to search for others. So he has become the national equivalent of a beloved family dog that never seems to get a boner until there is a state dinner. At function after function the guests must act as if they're not living in mortal fear that he's going to sniff crotches, hump legs, or pull one of the female diners aside to show her how he can "get the red out."

As the Lewinsky affair came into focus, it didn't take long to establish that she was young but not underage. She was an employee, not an intern. It seems she entered into her relationship with the president with her eyes open (insert your own stupid puns, I'm getting tired). In Lewinsky, Clinton found not a naive victim but someone else with a wounded psyche. Let's face it: no one with reasonable self-esteem brags of a childhood spent becoming an adroit liar. Monica is attracted to self-destruction in a way that Bill Clinton can appreciate. How else can you explain all those intimate conversations with failed DC careerist Linda Tripp's lapel? In Monica, Bill found a woman who can't believe he lets her touch him . . . you know, *down there*. For months the country has teetered on the brink of constitutional crisis because these two sexual retards are still astonished that if you rub it long enough, it will spit at you.

At first I thought Clinton was a goner, that Kenneth the Right-Winged Archangel would at least nail him on technicalities, that the president would drop in the polls and the Republican Congress would hound him from office. Shows you how much I know. Any blowjob comic worth his salt could have told you that all this was going to lead us to one unavoidable truth—*only about three Republicans are actually faithful to their spouses.* The rest of them created a silence so widespread that for weeks all that was audible on Capitol Hill was the sound of money changing hands.

I was also unaware of an ace up Clinton's sleeve: Americans are mesmerized by people with Southern drawls who behave in a sexually embarrassing fashion. They can't get enough of this. It's called *The Jerry Springer Show*. When the scandal hit, Clinton's ratings skyrocketed just like Springer's. I never saw it coming: I had been tuned to c-span.

So until this blows over, umm, peters out, oh, never mind . . . Anyway, I used to feel I stood a bit apart from most comics, because they discussed fellatio while I dissected public policy. Crotchgate has humbled me. I now defer to my foresighted comrades who have worked their entire careers toward this moment, when the country needs them for sage analysis of the most important issue of the day: the blowjob. Diceman, the floor is yours.

The United States no longer leads on international human-rights issues, according to Amnesty International. In other news, Saudi Arabia is not a good place for snow skiing.

A note written by Lincoln's assassin, John Wilkes Booth, sold at auction for $31,050. Where Jesse Helms got that kind of money is unknown.

Minnesota Gov. Jesse Ventura joined crews piling sandbags Thursday as residents of the Red River Valley fought to keep the river from overflowing emergency dikes. During a brief break from the effort Ventura lost an impromptu debate with one of the sandbags.

President Bush marked Thomas Jefferson's birthday in a ceremony at the White House Wednesday. Jefferson responded by having himself placed on a rotisserie to make spinning in his grave less difficult.

sixteen

The Clintons Are Coming!
The Clintons Are Coming!

When I read the words "Lake Skaneateles" in *Time*, I knew I had to get home. The name was as weird to me as "Ocean Atlantic" or the "University of Boston" because it's not Lake Skaneateles, it's Skaneateles Lake. I ought to know, I grew up in the town that shares the moniker nobody can pronounce.

Skanny-at-eh-less is how I was taught to say it, though many residents have bastardized it to Skinny-atlas. Nobody really cares that much how it's pronounced. Now that Skaneateles, New York has played host to President Bill Clinton, Candidate Hillary Clinton, First Daughter Chelsea Clinton, and First Dog Buddy Clinton for the final five days of their 1999 summer vacation, there is a good chance you have now heard of the place and that's good enough for most locals.

Unlike the obscurity it suffered when I was a kid, nowadays Skaneateles is occasionally newsworthy. Most recently, well-liked local man James "Jeff" Cahill brought the place to statewide attention when he freaked out and beat his wife, Jill, to the point of brain damage. Then, while out on bail, he disguised himself as an employee of Syracuse's University Hospital, where he finished her off with poison. Tried and convicted, the now not-well-liked Cahill has been sentenced to death.

But Cahill was an anomaly; usually the town makes news through whimsy. It used to host an annual short-and-fat-man race, and a few years ago it decided to market itself as a stress-free zone. Both brought national attention. Too bad Mr. Cahill failed to comply with the stress edict.

But a Clinton visit to Skaneateles to stay at swank lakeside digs owned by Tom and Kathy McDonald beat all the town's murders and Chamber of Commerce stunts put together. Having spent a few years on the campaign trail, I could estimate what was about to take place. After four or five New Hampshire primaries, you get pretty familiar with what happens when Goober meets Big Brother, or for that matter, Big Bubba. But estimates are sometimes wrong, so just to be sure, when the Clintons arrived on Monday, August 30, I was waiting.

"Skaneateles" is an Indian word that means, "beautiful lake surrounded by fascists." Well, it means something about a lake, anyway. Be prepared to jam your time machine in reverse if you want to talk politics with the locals in this tourist mecca 17 miles southwest of Syracuse.

Not since Skaneateles was part of the Underground Railroad has it come anywhere close to supporting progressive politics. Thanks to recent gains by Democrats, it's now three-to-one Republican. In his four successful presidential campaigns, Franklin Delano Roosevelt never once carried the town. Connecticut carpetbagger James Buckley, running on the Conservative ticket for the U.S. Senate in 1970, won in Skaneateles with his largest margin anywhere in the state.

I am almost always at odds with the consensus of opinion in Skaneateles. It's a pro-war, pro-death-penalty, anti-union kind of place. The worst of the town's politics are summarized thus: "I been nowhere, seen nothing, and hate everybody"

Only on environmental issues is there across-the-board semi-progressive thought in the Eastern Gateway to the Finger Lakes. You'd have to be completely deprived of all sensory awareness to fail to appreciate the splendor of nature in and around Skaneateles.

At the center of everything is the lake, 17 miles of the cleanest water in the Lower forty-eight. The glacially carved body bends to the east just about halfway down its length, providing ideal picture-postcard views from the rolling hills that surround it.

Each time I have returned, Skaneateles has been less recognizable. The Genesee and Jordan Street business district has slowly evolved from a few strips of stores that sold things everyday people needed to a collection of Christmas-tree-ornament shops run by Republican ladies on Prozac. And this time, I noticed, they'd moved the post office. I'm still woozy.

But what most depresses me when I return is the town's festering bigotry. Sometimes the locals' prejudice shines through even when they're offering a compliment. A few years back I was in town and having a drink at the Sherwood Inn, a lovely restaurant and tavern, when a patron spotted me and bellowed, "Jesus Christ, Barry, I seen you doing comedy on TV a few times. You're doing pretty well. You must have a big Jew agent."

I said, "Yeah he's six foot six—wears a forty-pound Star of David. I'm sure he could kick your ass."

Another time, at the same bar, while watching a Syracuse University basketball game, a couple of patrons referred to some players as "niggers" several times. I ran across the street and grabbed several free calendars from a pharmacy, ran back to the bar and distributed them to the bigoted patrons, saying, "I thought you might need these since you don't seem to know it's 1988."

Granted, most townsfolk are not overtly racist, but when confronted with overt racism, the tendency is to conspire in silence so the problem persists. And the bigots have no discretion—they simply presume I am also a bigot when they spew their hatred. (It's like in the old days, when total strangers would lay out lines of coke assuming that the best way to get to know someone was to commit a felony with them.) On the Sunday before the Clintons arrived, once again in the Sherwood, a man was muttering loudly about "Goddamned kikes." I was the only person who seemed to even notice the outburst.

The idea of the Clintons coming to Skaneateles conjured up irresistible visions of funny movies I saw at the long-gone Colonial Theatre when I was a kid. Films like *Bye-Bye Birdie*, *The Russians Are Coming! The Russians Are Coming!* and *After the Fox*—films in which small-town people suddenly become part of the bigger world they both covet and fear. In this case it was a matter of Democratic oil being poured on 17 miles of Republican water.

I am no fan of Bill Clinton's politics, but unlike most of his critics, I snipe from the left. I have no more use for the corporate-compromised, conscience-free trade initiating, welfare-reforming, Pentagon-growing, bombing-people-at-the-drop-of-his-pants policies than the next self-respecting political southpaw. But when reactionary crackpots accuse him of everything from treason to complicity in the Lindbergh kidnapping, I can't help but feel some sympathy for the enemy of my enemies.

And if Hillary Clinton were just half the threat to our way of life her detractors claim, I'd have long ago moved back to New York and begun working for her unannounced yet obvious U.S. Senate bid. Hillary isn't a radical-feminist rabble-rouser; she is a connected corporate mouthpiece. But I must say, I have on occasion agreed with her when almost everyone else scoffed at her remarks.

Last year, for example, Hillary claimed that there was a right-wing plot against the president. It doesn't take a paranoid imagination or a subscription to The *Washington Times* to realize that there has been a concerted and often far-fetched smear campaign against Bill Clinton. There were IMPEACH CLINTON bumper stickers before he took the oath of office. Because the president provided his detractors with so much viable mud to sling, it's simple work to make a mockery of anyone who would suggest that there was any sort of plot against the man.

So my first guess was that Hillary chose Skaneateles as a vacation destination not because she coveted retiring Senator Patrick J. Moynihan's job, but because she figured that after the national press corps had spent a week in my reactionary hometown, nobody could ever again question the existence of right-wing conspiracies.

When the Clinton trip was announced, local merchant Doug Clark seized the moment to announce, "If Bill and Hillary came to Doug's Fish Fry, I would refuse them service because they are intoxicated with power. And I could claim they appear to be intoxicated—I have a beer license. I just don't want them in my restaurant." This yokel actually thought he was being clever. Of course he had some support, but nearly everyone I spoke with made the same point—if the President of the United States wants to walk into your greasy fish fry, kiss his hem and cook the fish.

Clark didn't give up after his original remarks. He went on to posit that other bistro owners would cave in and serve the Clintons because they couldn't pass up the publicity. Media-shy Clark turned up on every network, several magazines, all the wire services, and major newspapers, thanks to his effort to make a principled stand against such weak-willed competitors. Clark blathered a lot about character during his brush with national notoriety.

Area residents first knew Doug Clark as the owner of a Syra-cuse joint called Doug's Working Man's Tavern. To promote his bar, Clark once had T-shirts printed that featured a picture of Doug and his partner kneeling Atlas-style, arms extended above them as each held up a gigantic naked breast. Of course this was twenty years ago, and so perhaps the George W. Bush statute of limitations saves the current guardian of village morals from prosecution for being a silly little hypocrite.

Actually, Clark made a fatal mistake when he took his politics public. He forgot that inexpensive fish dinners appeal as much to Democrats as to Republicans. For the first time in memory his restaurant did not have peak-season patrons lined up out the door.

I never thought I'd go to bat for a right-wing ex-cop but fair is fair, and one Skaneateles businessman deserves more distance from Clark than he has been afforded.

"I don't want to be tarred with the same brush [as Doug Clark]. I'm aware that the 1964 Civil Rights Law says you will serve who comes in your restaurant," said John Angyal, owner of Johnny Angel's. The former New York State trooper and Skaneateles judge spoke with me on Wednesday morning in his hamburger hall, just up Jordan Street from Doug's Fish Fry.

Angyal did rename his fried-bologna sandwich the Hillary Special in honor of the visit, but that was just a joke—not a great joke, but a joke. He sent Hillary Clinton a case of Johnny Angel's Heavenly Water, bottled from the lake, as a conciliatory gesture.

It was pretty funny having a guy who, when I was growing up, was one of the toughest cops in Central New York explain himself to me. He did a good job, Angyal's politics are far from mine, but he was St. Francis of Assisi when compared to Doug Clark.

Neither Clark nor Angyal's dining establishment received presidential visits, even though by Friday, when the Clintons made their last stop in town for ice cream at the Blue Water Chill (the stand in front of the Blue Water Grill), they'd hit almost every bistro in Skaneateles.

The Sherwood (which, despite my experiences with its patrons, has never demonstrated any support for racism or anti-Semitism) scored first on Monday night, when the Clintons surprised almost everyone, who assumed they'd stay in after their afternoon arrival, by showing up for dinner at 9 PM All the diners in the Sherwood were permitted to remain, but no one else was allowed through the door after the president arrived. By 11 PM I had joined several hundred people outside. Dozens squealed as if the Beatles had just taken the stage at Shea Stadium when the First Family finally emerged.

Most of the crowd had bet Bill and Hillary would be at Krebs up West Genesee Street, and each night Krebs became a scene of increasing hilarity as the Clintons avoided it. Krebs is an old-style restaurant that charges big money for a soup-to-nuts gorging of heavy dishes and rich desserts served on large platters Sunday-dinner-at Grandma's style. It has always attracted a ton of tourists (two tons when they leave), but it isn't the kind of place you go very often if you're interested in living much past fifty. The best thing about the place is the bar upstairs.

On Tuesday the First Family stayed in to eat pizzas that Bill picked up in person at Mark's Pizza.

About 9:10 PM on Wednesday I pulled around the corner up the street from Krebs (headed for that upstairs bar) and saw several hundred people swarming around the entrance. Krebs's front porch and yard were mobbed with people, cordoned off by ropes to keep the entrance clear and the gawkers off the street. State Police directed traffic and pedestrians. I stood in a crowd of maybe a hundred people across the street from the main crush. Although I didn't ask, a stranger volunteered, "With them Staties working the crowd and the ropes up, they're sure to be coming tonight."

"Here come the motorcycle cops!" an adolescent boy suddenly announced, provoking a collective explosion of joy from the throng.

"And there's the motorcade!!" bellowed a woman a good six inches from my right ear.

The motorcycles, several police cars, and an armada of sport utility vehicles whooshed past. From a brownish gold one Bill and Hillary Clinton waved at the crowd, which was now applauding furiously.

"Wooooooooooooooooo," whooped the people. Some began to laugh and congratulate one another for finally betting on the right restaurant. Inside, some patrons were eating their third humongous Krebs meal in as many nights, in hopes of being among the sequestered few to dine with the Clintons.

I wonder what they thought as the procession zoomed past Krebs and the "Wooooooooooooooooo's" turned to "Nooooooooooooooooo's." For the third consecutive night Krebs's staff and patrons, and the general public, had whiffed at Charlie Brown's football. The First Family dined at yupscale Rosalie's Cucina that evening. Most of the gawkers took it in good spirit; even if the Clintons hadn't arrived, at least they had driven past.

On Thursday night, when all hope had been abandoned at Krebs, Bill and Hillary Clinton walked in. They didn't have the big meal. He had a peach dessert and she had soup. Obviously they had read newspaper accounts that reported one of the owners in tears when they didn't come on Wednesday. So on Thursday, after fundraisers in Cazenovia and Syracuse, on a night when their schedule appeared to be crammed as full as the average Krebs patron, they paid their respects to the landmark.

There were some protesters in Skaneateles during the Clinton stay. One group was lobbying for "The freedom to protect the U.S. flag from physical desecration." Legislative desecration of the Bill of Rights did not seem to concern these folks.

There was also an antiabortion group that was barking rosaries in the park with such hostility that it almost sounded as if they were cops shouting instructions at Jesus's mother. "Hail Mary, full of grace . . . blessed be thy name! Freeze!"

None of these people were even from Skaneateles. The locals kept their complaints minimal—most of the dissention came in the form of T-shirts carrying double-entendre messages like "Skaneateles, New York 1999—Clinton Slept Here . . . TOO!" Clever.

But for every T-shirt salesman there were five hundred people who were charmed silly by the Clintons. Sixty seconds after the First Family got out of their SUV at the McDonald estate my eleven-year-old goddaughter, Bridget Huxford, not only met and shook hands with all three of them, she had the president's autograph to boot. She was one of the first of many locals to be flattened by the gracious Clinton steamroller.

To put it in the Republican parlance, the town grew kinder and gentler toward the Clintons as each day passed. Bill, Hillary, and Chelsea had been accessible to the townsfolk and supportive of local businesses. Most everyone admitted that the presidential visit was exciting and had gone well. Some even cautiously felt that it had done the wealthy little town some good. Most shocking of all were the appearance of several lawn signs in support of Hillary's senate candidacy.

Mrs. Clinton is already endearing herself to a voter base that can be found in every precinct and ward in New York state— women. They like her more than they may ever let on to husbands who have annoyed them and betrayed them just like Hillary's has annoyed and betrayed her. After watching the Clintons charm good behavior out of my hometown, I made Hillary a near odds-on favorite to be moving to New York only to move back to Washington.

In the end the Clintons were about as intimidated by my hometown as I would be by Hope, Arkansas. They understood that these days even Republicans are more swayed by *People* magazine than by the *National Review*. They took to the area so well, and were so well received, that I half suspected they might buy a place ten miles up the west side of the lake, in a hamlet called New Hope. Alas, before they left Skaneateles they opted to relocate to Westchester County and a $1.7 million shack in Chappaqua.

And though the Clinton's upstate adventure may have lacked glamour, it did have impact. When Bill and Hill, Chel and Bud waved goodbye and climbed aboard Air Force One at Syracuse's Hancock Field at 2:17 Friday afternoon, Skaneateles had gone from the town with the name nobody could pronounce to the town with the name everybody couldn't pronounce.

A Yugo running on lighter fluid would have a better chance of driving nonstop from Nova Scotia to Argentina than Dick Cheney's heart has of making it to 2004.

Everyone who wants to join the NRA should be shot. If they survive and still think it's a good idea, we'll know it was a head wound.

Secretary of State Designate Colin Powell has called for expanding the number of minority Americans in U.S. posts overseas. Senators Jesse Helms (Fungal infection–NC) and Strom Thurmond (Raptor–SC) immediately endorsed the idea and offered to help send as many African-Americans abroad as possible.

seventeen

Memory Lane

When the First Family put Skaneateles, New York, on the map, they removed me from another.

On the last Friday night in June 1970, the last day of my junior year in high school, I drove my mother's 1965 Buick Lesabre convertible down Coon Hill Road. As I approached the "T" at East Lake Road, I hit the brakes, but they failed, so I cruised right through the stop sign and across the often busy road. Praise Allah, there was no traffic. The car struck a cast-iron New York State highway sign, which sheered off and sliced through the roof on the passenger's side at such an angle that it would have decapitated anyone riding shotgun. Anyone in the back seat would have succumbed to massive chest injuries caused by the sign and/or the shotgun rider's head.

The vehicle then plunged off a cement drainpipe culvert that acted as a ramp to propel me over several trees before finally coming to rest on the remains of a large oak that had been snapped in two.

The irony escaped me as I sat and listened to the Supremes finish singing "STOP! In the Name of Love" on the still functioning radio before dropping through the window to the ground and hiking back to the road. A neighbor ran up to me and asked, I kid you not, if I had seen the *plane crash*.

I knew nothing of aviation disasters but wondered if he might help me pull my car out because I had gotten stuck. Just then my friend Mitch Slater pulled up, and I told him my car was hung up.

He asked, "Where?"

I said, "In there," pointing to the dark smoking crater carved in the trees.

Mitch was incredulous "In THERE? Was anyone with you?"

"No."

Then the neighbor ran off to call the cops. A few seconds later another friend, Peter Wuerslin, pulled up and I'd told him what I told everyone, I said I was stuck. Wuerslin, a high school football teammate and pal looked at Slater's vw pulled off to the side of the road and said, "There? No problem!"

But as I walked back to the wreckage I heard Pete conferring with Mitch and asking "What? All the way in THERE?"

Pete followed me down to the car and with urgency inquired, "Crim, this is important. Was *anyone* with you?"

I was still hopeful, "No, nobody was with me, do you think we can get this out of here?"

Pete gasped as he reached the car's remains, shook his head and said, "It's in bad shape."

"Well, maybe we can find an all-night mechanic," I pleaded.

Wuerslin gave it to me straight. "No all-night mechanic can help, Crim. We have gotten out of a lot of things, but there is no way around this one. That car is totaled, you're lucky to be alive."

As I thought of my parent's reaction to me destroying their car on the very day I had received my Blue Card signifying that I had passed driver's education, I was not so sure. It was a long weekend as I awaited their return from a wedding in Connecticut. The hell I caught when they arrived was nowhere near as bad as the anticipation of it had been.

I was in an odd state of limbo for the thirty-six hours between the accident and my parents' arrival. There was great feeling of dread but also teenage notoriety for totaling the car that had become a major attraction up at the Evans Brothers service station. As wrecks went, it was rated as the worst anyone had ever seen that had caused no injuries.

Good thing I was wearing my seatbelt.

Eventually I paid eight dollars worth of fines for being an *unsupervised learner* and passing a stop sign. My day in court was saved when my father said he feared that a criminal record could hinder my chances of joining the service. The judge, grim-faced and stern up until that moment, softened and said that he didn't want to be the one who impeded my opportunity to serve in Vietnam.

Yikes! *How often did these people think I could cheat death?*

For lowering the case of the "T" at Coon Hill and Route 41, a portion of my name became part of Skaneateles lore. Thereafter my friends referred to the section of wilderness that I deforested as "Crim Lane." Never again would they look at that particular chunk of real estate and think of anything more exciting than my enormous blunder.

Never again, that is, until the Clintons came and stayed at the foot of Coon Hill Road at the beautiful beach home of Tom and Kathy McDonald. Fortunately the posh estate wasn't there in 1970, because a new phone pole carrying electrical and communications lines to the McDonald home would have been directly on the driver's side of the LeSabre. Had I struck that pole, I wouldn't have lived to see Bubba tame the Goobers.

And now that Skaneateles is on the map, can an all-night mechanic be far behind?

Actual exchange between Barry and another American in a bar in Managua, Nicaragua, in 1988:

> AMERICAN: Walk around these streets and tell me how these people can live this way.

> BARRY: I'm pretty sure it's because we have most of their stuff.

If W were put on any shorter leash, he'd be wearing Cheney's pants.

A vote for Nader was a vote for Bush. A vote for Bush was a vote for Bush. Even a vote for Buchanan was a vote for Bush. And yet he still had to cheat to win.

eighteen

Flag-Waiving

I understand that many took comfort in the American flag after 9/11. They saw it as a symbol of resilience, determination and respect for victims of terror. They also viewed it as an endorsement of the thousands who were doing all they could to clear wreckage and search against hope for even one more survivor.

To fly the flag and wear red, white, and blue allowed people to make a gesture of sympathy and stand in solidarity against the heinous criminals who planned and committed the horrific massacres on September 11, 2001. I understand and applaud the human decency such gestures represent.

But I couldn't join in the nationalistic fervor because I feared it would lead to more senseless death and because it was inarticulate. No one who was killed on September 11 died for the red, white, and blue. They perished trying to earn a living for themselves and their families. Or they died with compassionate courage in heroic efforts to save lives. The flag-waving came after that. I repeat, most of it was completely sincere. People were in pain and needed to grab hold of something. Flags are easy to hold.

I have another view of the flag. It emanates from a context that is unique to me. It certainly is a view that many despise. I wish I didn't know what I do because then I could just put on the colors and not risk having people think that because I won't embrace a current mass symbol of compassion, hope, and resistance to madness, that I somehow cared less for the victims than the flag-wavers.

It was because of victims that I couldn't cling to the flag, a symbol of all sorts of heinous crimes committed by this country. I used to try to embrace Old Glory because, as an American, it belonged to me as well. And because I love my country. But as Mark Twain said, that "comes naturally, like breathing. There is no personal merit in breathing."

One day in the summer of 1988, sitting in a plane at the airport in Tegucigalpa on the way home from Central America, I saw a giant U.S. Air Force transport (I think they are called C-130's). It sat on the runaway with its large cargo bay agape. The plane was empty, but the area surrounding it was littered with its military cargo. Because of where I had just been, I knew it was earmarked to spread more heartbreak and carnage upon the peasants of the region. This was because the U.S. government, in support of multinational corporations, wanted to keep the prices of commodities as cheap as possible. And they were busy cheapening the most important commodity of all, human life. That plane contained support and endorsement for the death squads that were combing the countryside and terrorizing the populace of Guatemala, Honduras, El Salvador, and Nicaragua.

Death squads were CIA-trained terrorists that murdered and tortured people suspected of having allegiance to anyone but United States-backed dictators or "contras" in the region. The murders they committed were often excruciatingly gruesome because they were meant to terrorize others to keep them from joining the battle for land reform and human rights.

Painted on the tailfin of that transport was a big American flag. I sat there and considered how many more lives would be destroyed because of the state-sponsored terrorism that would be implemented with the commodities that had been unloaded from that one plane. I thought of how this evil was being done at the expense of U.S. taxpayers. I knew that they'd never permit such a thing to happen if they only understood what was being done in their name and in the murky shadow of the Stars and Stripes. I thought about how the money that was being spent on barbarism would be looked upon as foreign aid. That sanitary little term could delude Americans into believing, when they saw the figures for this "aid," that the USA was philanthropic and the world was not sufficiently grateful. I sadly mulled over how the whole scam was cynically packaged as an attempt to export democracy to backward people. In fact, it was an effort to negate the will of the majority down there.

Eventually it succeeded.

Sitting on that runway in far off Tegucigalpa, the flag left my possession, for good. Never again could I wear it or endorse it, because never again would it *not* symbolize what I knew had been done in Central America.

I have lived a flagless life for many years now and risk the disdain of my fellow Americans because of it. After the 9/11 attacks numerous people, some of them old friends, told me that they thought my inability to fall in behind the flag and the flag-waving Bush Administration reflected poorly upon me. I understand why they might have felt that way, and I am sorry to have disappointed them. But because I have seen the flag used to spread terror, I cannot risk betraying the victims of terror, just because I fear some people will mistakenly believe my heart is not in shreds over the 9/11 human calamity.

I still believe in what this country can be. Essential to the continued quest for the American dream is free speech. One thing I am free to say is that I want to end the massacre of all innocents. I want no more terror. I also say, by not flying the flag, that our problems can't be solved through nationalism. I say that nationalism can be found at the source of much of the madness that has changed our world in such an awful way. That said, I understand why so many people clung to Old Glory after 9/11. I know that they did so out of compassion and decency. I respect them for that, and I defend their right to choose that symbol at that moment. I hope that at least some of them understand that other good and decent people might have some pretty good reasons for seeking a different path toward healing the enormous wound we sustained.

"Operation Iron Hammer" is the name the U.S. military has given its new crackdown on Iraqi insurgents. Excuse me, but aren't hammers supposed to be made of *steel*?

Then again, if you can build a rationale for war from fluff and create a quagmire from desert, why not make a hammer from iron?

Nazis originally coined the term "Operation Iron Hammer." It was used in a campaign meant to smash the Soviet Union. So the Pentagon has chosen not just a stupid name but a *fascist, losing, stupid name.* So maybe it is appropriate. (According to MSNBC's website: "Eisenhammer," the German for "iron hammer," was a Luftwaffe code name for a plan to destroy Soviet [power] generating plants in the Moscow and Gorky areas in 1943.")

"Operation Rubber Hammer" would be more appropriate because the policy will undoubtedly bounce back and smash Bush in the nose.

"Operation Ironhead" would be a good name for the Bush administration's foreign policy initiatives. Like iron, the initiatives are soft yet dense.

nineteen

Axis of Weasels

On Friday, February 8, 2002, W entered the inaugural proceedings at an Olympiad that was built and funded in a manner that could make Arthur Andersen himself pinken with embarrassment. Who better than our twitchy office-taker-in-chief to welcome an assembled mass that would spend the next few weeks averting its gaze from the greed, graft, and corruption that helped bring the Downhill Cumorah Pageant to Mormon City, U S A? After locally flavoring the international gathering with some traditional American jingoistic remarks, Dubster made his way to his place among the U.S. delegation.

Seventeen-year-old figure skater Sasha Cohen randomly chose the seat reserved for the court-appointed president. As she moved over to make room for the world's most eloquent argument against nepotism, Cohen apologized for being such meager company for a world leader. Bush graciously said that he couldn't think of any better companion for the festivities.

Cohen, who was speaking with her mother via cell phone, excitedly told Mom of her suddenly plum seating assignment. Emboldened by his friendliness, Sasha asked Bush if he'd say hello to her mother, a Ukrainian immigrant. He did. He then assured the flabbergasted mom that her daughter was behaving very well. Whether or not Mrs. Cohen asked Bush to keep his own younger female relations away from Sasha until she had passed any Olympic drug tests was not disclosed.

Cohen, already a very recognizable member of the high profile United States figure skating squad, immediately graduated to media-darling status. The story of her encounter with Dubyahoo burnt up the newswires. Video of the cell-phone chat bounced off satellites and into homes all over the world.

The next day a breathless Cohen was taken to do an interview with NBC's Bob Costas. This was when the most indelible moment of the Salt Lake Games occurred. After recounting those parts of the story we had already heard too many times, Cohen added a detail for NBC that had escaped earlier coverage. She told Costas that she had asked the president if he planned to stay and watch any of the athletic events. Bush said he couldn't because "I have a war to fight."

You're cringing now, aren't you?

It is unclear whether or not he added "Little lady," to his swaggering exit line. It is a matter of public record that the great warrior then boarded Air Force One and flew to the Wyoming front to address his troops in Jackson Hole.

The image of Bush using John Wayne rhetoric on a fawning adolescent paints a creepy picture that will always be synonymous with the Salt Lake Games. Here was a man running a war effort, justified by the murder of innocents, that had now killed many more unoffending people than were lost on September 11. Throughout the ordeal Bush has played the crisis for political advantage. Hiding behind a logic-proof red, white and blue shield, Bush has pushed to:

- liberate corporations from reasonable scrutiny (goodbye worker rights and environmental standards);

- increase repression of dissent;

- pass yet another tax giveaway to the rich while the nation deficit-spends on munitions, corporate welfare, and police state fortifications.

During his State of the Union Address last month, W declared World War on Iran, Iraq and North Korea. In the speech he called the three nations an Axis of Evil. With the Taliban banished and Moby bin Laden either dead or receiving dialysis treatments from Lex Luthor in some high-tech cavern, W decided it was time to imply that these three wildly disparate nations had joined a ludicrously improbable alliance of evil that required immediate and violent dispersal.

No matter how lifelike his handlers made him seem, and regardless of his pre-fabbed new threats, Bush's true purpose for cacophonous saber rattling was obvious. It was meant to obscure the growing din of the Take the Money Enron scandal, a scam in which Bush's own Axis of Weasels (note: term coined by B C almost a year before reactionaries pinned it on France, Germany, etc.) is deeply implicated.

Not since Ronald Reagan have we had a president who is as stupid as he is evil. This explains how Bush devised and delivered his cornball yet toxic farewell to Sasha Cohen. Only a preposterously pompous dope could tell someone, even a fawning seventeen-year-old, "I have a war to fight" and then strut off. Even worse, this self-deluded nincompoop made the statement knowing that he had a public record of avoiding real combat in Vietnam by hiding in, and at times *from*, the Texas National Guard back in the 1970s. His daddy squirreled (and that is the proper verb) him away in a Guard unit peppered with the sons of Big Brother.

His father was reupped as a human shield with the recent concealment of Junior's Texas gubernatorial papers at the George Bush Presidential Library and Museum at Texas A & M University. The cloaked documents would likely demonstrate that the Bush Axis of Weasels has been a wholly owned subsidiary of Enron for a very long time. If an upcoming court battle over the papers looks like it could lead to Texas's tight freedom-of-information laws actually getting enforced, don't be surprised if one of A & M's infamous pep rally bonfires tragically consumes the Bush Library.

The utter shamelessness concentrated in the "I have a war to fight" comment provoked a genuine Vietnam combat vet friend of mine to respond, "That Mickey Mouse sonofabitch is lucky he never made it to Nam, because he is exactly the kind of chickenshit ocs grad who real combat vets fragged on his first trip to the latrine. 'I have a war to fight!' What an asshole! Idiots like that get a lot of people killed. Nope, he wouldn't have lasted long, and Charlie wouldn't have had *a thing* to do with it."

Thirty years after avoiding a fatal bowel movement in Southeast Asia, George W. Bush has the U.S. military firing live ammunition with deadly results. To the Axis of Weasels, collateral damage is just a pleasant byproduct of its ability to create an international distraction with the world's most lethal flare guns. If not for this ever-escalating battle with a shadowy and exaggerated enemy, Bush could well find himself being gaveled out of office just the way he was gaveled in. And then we would be spared stories of how this shifty little guy tries to impress girls by portraying himself as a single-handed he-man war fighter.

In each stage-managed appearance Bush sells his war against an axis here and an evildoer there as if his measly political life depends on it—because it does. Whenever GWB can get an impressionable child to speak of his sordid endeavor as if *his truth is marching on*, it means more time has been bought to shred and disconnect himself from a scandal that engulfs him right up to his beady little eyeballs.

So even though Bush left the Olympics so he could confab with the power elite in an exclusive resort, he foisted bombast on a child about heading off to war. This is infuriating because had W been anywhere near the violence he so desperately wants to escalate, you know he'd have ordered Air Force One from Utah to

Nebraska or Poppy's Library or a National Guard Unit assigned to keep us safe from incursions by the Mexican Air Force. And he would have stayed in seclusion until Andy or Gomer or Cheney told him it was safe to come out again.

George W. Bush has a war to fight!
And I have a lunch to lose.

Bush looked so reverent when they played "God Save the Queen" at the state dinner at Buckingham Palace because he thought the anthem was in honor of *J. Edgar Hoover.*

It was outrageous that the cancelled CBS miniseries implied that Nancy and Ronald Reagan spoke ill of gays. They didn't speak ill of gays, they just *shook them down for Nancy's wardrobe.*

It's been discovered that two trailers alleged to have been Iraqi WMD mobile production facilities were instead used for filling weather balloons with helium. Unless the Bush administration wants to make a case that Saddam liked to order WMD production while using a Donald Duck voice, the Bushists have once again struck sand.

twenty

An Activist's Lament

I am frequently accused of being a Red, and when it happens, I try to foster the belief, because Americans have to learn that people have a perfect right to be a Red or anything else they desire or just happen to be. So when asked if I'm a Commie (or gay or unpatriotic or what have ya), I always respond by saying, "I'm whatever threatens you!" But the truth is, I'm not a Red because I could never take the meetings.

The so-called progressive political movement is too often paralyzed by process and petty turf wars, fought by people who have more time, and fewer other things to do, than anyone else.

How many times have you attended the first meeting of many people concerned about an issue, only to spend the entire evening watching a few people debate how that and future meetings should be conducted? The next meeting is less well attended, but the original adversaries are back, armed with even more verbose arguments. Eventually almost no one shows up. The people who didn't return to later meetings were not lacking in social conscience, they simply didn't have time for what was, in essence, group therapy dominated by a few needy blowhards.

Happily, this doesn't describe every group and every cause. Sadly, it describes far too many of them. Under the guise of democracy, progressives spend too much time hearing out emotionally challenged political allies as they discuss how much they distrust the rest of their political allies. If you tire of hearing about mistrust and unbelievably petty grievances and say so, then your commitment to the cause is questioned. But really, you only spoke up because while these people were acting on their petty indifferences, bombs were still falling, workers were still getting screwed over, innocent people were still living under tyrants, bigotry was still running amuck, and the environment was still being destroyed.

In over thirty years of political activism I have never seen a war stopped, a river saved, or dictator deposed because someone at a meeting of progressives prefaced remarks with "I have some personal issues that I think are really important to share with you before we get too far along . . ."

I say this with no ill feeling toward anyone but because I believe it's time progressives understood that if we can't get out of our own way, we're never going to change the world.

Ari Fleischer is leaving his job as the mouthpiece for the court-appointed Bush administration. The country hasn't suffered a reversal this profound since the XFL folded.
Fleischer will leave some mighty big clown shoes to fill.

The software used for electronic voting is different from most. When its manufacturers get a prompt that reads, "This program has been corrupted," they know it's ready to be sent to election officials.

Funny how Republicans become environmental conservationists when it comes to paper trails for ballots. These people who drive a Humvee to the end of the driveway to get the mail suddenly don't think it's a good idea to waste the paper and ink it would take to verify election returns.

twenty-one

Torture Stalks MSNBC Viewers!

I don't get much news from television these days.

But then, neither does anyone else.

On the morning of Wednesday, April 3, 2002, I made the mistake of turning on the TV in search of information about the madness in the Middle East. I started with CNN, but saccharine-induced nausea seemed a high price to pay for chitchat from happy people lounging around an absurd living room-news set.

I jumped to C-SPAN, where a paranoid Republican caller had the floor, which was warping badly. I checked C-SPAN II, where reporters sucking up to some Pentagon slick at a news briefing drove me off.

MSNBC was next. I knew this was dicey. The GE-Gates Net actually features a show called "Alan Keyes Is Making Sense." To whom? Moonies freebasing LSD? But it was MSNBC or "Fair and Balanced" Fox News (not to be confused with self-effacing and generous-of-spirit Rush Limbaugh), so I gambled on MSNBC.

I lost.

The first thing I saw was Ashleigh Banfield, the finest electronic journalist this side of Stone Phillips, wandering around a hospital parking lot in what should be Palestine. Until I saw all of her protective gear, I hadn't realized that MSNBC has an Armored News Division. She looked farcical in a flak jacket that could have easily doubled as a futon. "PRESS" was written across her chest. She also sported an oversized helmet emblazoned front and back with "TV" as she interviewed several grieving Palestinian women adorned in gauzy protective scarves.

In Banfield's defense, Israeli forces seem to have the same sort of trouble discerning journalists and other innocents from terrorists that U.S. forces have differentiating Red Crosses from bullseyes. Still, standing there with unprotected Palestinians, wearing everything but a frying pan on her head, she loaned a certain Monty Pythonesque air to the proceedings.

Post-9/11 Banfield is to journalism what George W. Bush is to statesmanship. They are both Texas-rooted lightweights (she was a Dallas talking head, he was just a head) who've been deified by a scared and scarred nation, devoid of credible information and leadership. America used to get Edward R. Murrow and FDR. Now it's someone to whom hair color is an issue and a guy who only fears fear itself when Omaha is fogged in.

Despite Banfield's comical appearance and relentless dedication to advancement in the Cult of Personality, her story was compelling and heart-rending because of its inescapable specific gravity.

She spoke with several emotionally devastated survivors of people about to be buried in a mass grave in the hospital parking lot. The corpses had piled too high inside, and public health was endangered by so much rotting flesh. It was a terrible situation. Footage showed a backhoe breaking up the concrete in the parking lot and then digging the grave. Pallets of shrouded dead were in evidence. Across the way, in Israel, similar heartbreak had occurred again and again in recent weeks. Violence was begetting violence. The Grim Reaper was working all the OT he wanted. Sadness and futility crushed me into my chair, frozen under the weight of the world.

Banfield wrapped up her report and threw it back to MSNBC studio anchors Alex Witt and Rick Sanchez. Sanchez said something about it's being a "great story." I couldn't believe someone could employ a superlative after seeing a tale of such boundless grief and horror. But then, this was my first dose of Rick Sanchez.

Within the next few segments Sanchez demonstrated that he is a media post-9/11 wonder. He's quick to editorialize, smugly supportive of the Purported War on Terror, and always interrupting what little information trickles from other MSNBC staffers and guests. Cable news has become a word-association test for dopes like Sanchez.

Holding up a headline from a New York tabloid about violence in Bethlehem, he expressed outrage by bellowing, "BETHLE-HEM—WHERE JESUS WAS BORN!" Now there was something we needed in a story about the Middle East—religious zealotry from a news anchor.

Another editorial comment came during a story about wide-scale regional protests against Sharon's assault on Palestinians. A camera cut to Muammar al-Qaddafi at a Libyan demonstration and Sanchez scoffed something to the effect of "no surprise he's there." This courageous journalist isn't one to miss a chance to demonize someone his audience already reviles.

The capper came when Sanchez actually endorsed torture of United States-held prisoners by having allied governments do the dirty work. "The Egyptians have been known to torture people and get pretty good information," he offered cheerily.

Maybe so, but then again, it's torture watching Rick Sanchez, and you get pretty bad information.

An ex-CIA agent (I missed his name because by this point I was retching pretty violently) served as the voice of reason in the torture interview. The former spy suggested that you couldn't trust information provoked by torture. This obviously disappointed Sanchez, who then tried to rally by puzzling over why we should be concerned that the rest of the Arab world would be upset with de-facto U.S torture of Purported War on Terror prisoners. The CIA guy paid lip service to maintaining ethical standards. Sanchez scoffed again. Then the mole said, "Bush needs to keep his war alliance happy." This finally caused the light bulb to click above Sanchez' thick anchor head. Relieved, he said, "Oh, *I* get it—P R."

That's right, Rick, torture equals bad public relations. See "Inquisition, The." That was when a bunch of people, who thought BETHLEHEM, WHERE JESUS WAS BORN was an important place, committed atrocities against innocents. Hundreds of years later they're still getting bad P R.

I turned off the T V but remembered the name, Rick Sanchez. This new-breed news anchor candidly expresses his reactionary ignorance and, because of it, his days with M S N B C are numbered. Sooner or later the Pentagon is going to need a new spokesperson.

Who drew up Bush's "road map to peace?" *Wrongway Peachfuzz?*

Getting directions to peace from George W. Bush is the equivalent of having George Steinbrenner draw up a plan for running a baseball franchise on a shoestring.

Here's a tip for travelers on the road toward peace: If you run into George W. Bush *anywhere* along the way, you are headed in the wrong direction.

twenty-two

Justice Deferred:
Dirty Deed, Dirty Deal

Remember those old George Booth cartoons of the long-bearded, raggedy prisoner chained to a dungeon wall because he had offended some totalitarian authority? Well, so does John Ashcroft, who has now successfully integrated that image into the American legal system.

Speaking from Moscow, where I presume he had traveled to lay a wreath on Joseph Stalin's grave, Kaiser Ashcroft disclosed that the Justice Department had broken up an Al Qaeda plot to detonate a radioactive "dirty bomb" inside the United States. Abdullah al-Muhajir, a thirty-one-year-old American citizen born in Brooklyn as Jose Padilla, has been detained in the case.

The word "arrested" was used, but since the Justice Department feels no need to file charges or make a case, "detained" is more accurate.

According to the usa Patriot Act of 2001, Abdullah al-Muhajir needn't be charged with anything for the duration of the Purported War on Terrorism. In other words, so long as there is a terrorist on planet Earth, this American citizen is relegated to rot in confinement with no defense, trial, or contact with the outside world.

According to the usa Patriot Act, trials are not patriotic. This law, rushed through Congress in the post-9/11 haze, is just as Orwellian as its bombastic name implies. According to this horrendous piece of legislation, the American citizenry has no right to an open examination of the case against Abdullah al-Muhajir, or anyone else the government chooses to label as a terrorist. We have no right to learn his side of the story. We have no right to sit in a jury box and determine the validity of this case. We have no right to the details of what could be a very serious threat to public safety.

Whether or not that threat to our safety comes from a dirty nuclear device or a police state—or both—we may never know.

Actually, we do know that under the court-appointed Bush regime, the ever-shrinking Bill of Rights will soon be reduced to the Second Amendment. It's a relief to consider that no matter how horribly this right-wing band of yahoos defaces the principles of our country, we will still be permitted to buy guns with which to shoot ourselves and escape an ever-more-miserable state of affairs.

The following day headlines trumpeted the dirty-bomb story by telling us that a terrorist plot had been "foiled." The convenient thing about the Bush, Cheney & Ashcroft Railroad is that that we no longer have to waste a lot of time using qualifying terms like "alleged." Nor are we expected to express any doubts as the Authoritarian Express screams past us, right on tightly guarded schedule.

Abdullah al-Muhajir was detained on May 8, 2002, but Ashcroft didn't see fit to announce this until over a month later, from the bosom of Mother Russia. This makes it much tougher for us to get answers to questions Ashcroft has no intention of answering.

For instance:

- If this person was arrested on May 8, why didn't we hear about it on May 8? What possible harm could have come from informing us of this man's detainment? It's not as if such a disclosure could compromise the case, because the United States isn't bothering to make one.

- Who is in charge of announcing arrests at the Justice Department? The same person who schedules cable-TV-service calls?

- How many more unconvicted people are rotting in American jails, not awaiting trials?

- Isn't the timing of this announcement just a tad suspect, since it comes on the heels of all sorts of disclosures about 9/11 intelligence failures that have embarrassed the court-appointed Bush administration? (Or would have, if it were capable of feeling embarrassment.)

- Has anyone in the former Soviet Union thanked the court-appointed Bush administration for vindicating the KGB by using it as a template for the Office of Homeland Security?

- Does it shame you at all to consider that the Catholic Church is now more open and accessible than the Justice Department?

- What ever became of writs of habeas corpus? Are they being stored in the same pit where Dick Cheney's appointment book lurks?

- Doesn't the public have a right to know the details about plots against it?

- Might not this detainment make a martyr of a man who could otherwise be shown, in a fair and public trial, to be deserving of long-term penal confinement?

And those are just a few queries. I'm sure there are many, many more that will never be answered by the arrogant church-state integrationist who is America's highest-ranking legal officer.

Osama bin Laden is reportedly trying to destroy the American way of life, but he's a lightweight compared to John Ashcroft and the rest of the court-appointed Bush administration. We don't know if America was targeted with a dirty bomb (and nobody has any intention of proving it), but we do know that our judicial system is now reeling from the shock waves of a dirty deal.

Americans do not require the protection of tyrants and their police-state tactics. We need protection *from* them. With an assist from an ill-advised piece of legislation, George W. Bush and John Ashcroft are destroying those protections and telling us that it's for our own good.

This is pathological nonsense.

If Abdullah al-Muhajir is guilty, prove it in a court of law. This man is entitled to the best possible legal representation, and then a jury of his fellow Americans should decide his guilt or innocence. By doing this, we could show the world that, at least in this case, we are a free and fair nation.

Until that happens, we have returned to what Mark Twain once derided as the United States of Lyncherdom.

"It's untidy. And freedom's untidy. And free people are free to make mistakes and commit crimes and do bad things." —Doomsday Don Rumsfeld, unintentionally disclosing that some of the freest people in the world are now occupying 1600 Pennsylvania Avenue.

For those of you who missed the State of the Union Address there's good news: Pfizer will reissue it as its annual report.

If you believe that the air strikes on al Jazeera headquarters in Iraq and (previously) Afghanistan were a coincidence, you probably think that Pat Buchanan was the popular choice among Jews in Florida in 2000.

Hey, if al Jazeera didn't want to be bombed, then why did they give the U.S. military their Global Positioning Satellite coordinates?

The Pentagon thinks "al Jazeera" is Arabic for "bullseye."

The U.S. military planned for months (OK, years) to become an occupying force in the Middle East, but it's surprised by suicide-bomber tactics? Apparently we need to take a second look at the backs of the Hooters menus upon which Tampa Tommy Franks drew up his plans for this operation.

Do you get the feeling that were CNN's Paula Zahn born fifty years earlier, she'd have done voiceover work for Leni Riefenstahl?

Leave it to Geraldo Rivera *to get booted out of a theater of war for histrionics.*

They say the devil is in the details, and there were details working night and day at the Abu Ghraib Prison.

twenty-three

Pox Americana

Your flag decal won't get you
into heaven anymore
we're already overcrowded
from your dirty little war
Now Jesus don't like killing
no matter what the reasons for
and your flag decal won't get you
into heaven anymore

—John Prine

On January 21, 2003, the United States reached a significant milestone when it passed the halfway mark of the court-appointed Bush administration. A hardy sort, Americans had survived two years and a day of excruciating corruption, skullduggery, and embarrassment. Several million lucid people marked this sad anniversary at peace rallies. These gatherings were largely ignored and/or dismissed by a corporate media that beat an electronic war drum that provided George W. Bush with the cacophonous distraction he required to defy logic, decency, and constitutional law—all prerequisites for marching foolishly into military conflict in Iraq.

As war loomed, Bush's rationales for it faded faster than newsprint in a greenhouse. Each alleged Iraqi smoking gun turned to licorice. So many intelligence documents were fudged that Cuba feared it would be the next to be invaded, if only for its sugar. Saddam and Al Qaeda each had more plausible links to George W. Bush than one another. Iraqi weapons of mass destruction (a term Bush expanded to include anything more lethal than a whoopee cushion) were everywhere, but nowhere.

Much of the cost of Bush's inevitable war was to be tacked on to the already obscene $400 billion dollar Pentagon budget. The new Department of Fatherland Security advised us to go out and buy duct tape and plastic sheeting to protect our homes from chemical attack: $400 billion PLUS per year for alleged defense PLUS whatever the gargantuan homeland security apparatus cost, but we were supposed to run down to True Value to buy *duct tape* to ensure our safety. Unfortunately, a very effective countermeasure to duct tape and plastic sheeting is *a box cutter*, bringing us back to square one via a very expensive route.

Throughout a savage winter Bush considered exactly zero outside opinions as he stuck his head in the sand about his war in the desert. No matter how much bottled water Halliburton had to airlift, he was hell-bent for quagmire. W's perpetual blathering about his desire to bring democracy to Iraq was contradicted by his abject refusal to acknowledge that other heads of state opposed his war at the behest of large and vocal majorities of their own constituents.

Winter had become so pornographic that upstate New York cable companies considered moving the Weather Channel to pay-per-view before the polar siege finally relented in late March 2003. That's when the winds abated, the sun came out and the temperature zoomed into the sixties—so of course that was exactly when George W. Bush decided to attack Iraq.

The day after the war began I headed to Boston for some business and pleasure. I forget the business details, but the pleasure came because of a kindness done for me by my friend, Boston radio legend Charles Laquidara. Charles made a call and arranged some great tickets for me to see the Syracuse Orangemen's first two NCAA Men's Basketball Tournament games at the Fleet Center in Beantown. (A tournament my beloved Orangemen would win a few weeks later in New Orleans. The night they were crowned I sent out an e-mail to friends that stated simply, "I'm drinking heavily and both cars are on fire." This was an exaggeration. I don't have two cars.)

And so, on the second full day of war, I drove out Route 17 to Binghamton, where I picked up I-88 and jutted up to catch I-90 into Boston. I listened to radio war coverage until I felt colicky, and then turned it off for most of the ride.

Normally I'd have felt gleeful heading for fun in my artistic hometown, especially since I was making the trip across dry pavement with the windows open for the first time since October. Plus it's a really beautiful drive starting with the more accessible rolling views of upstate New York and then up and over the Berkshires, just splendid. Somewhere along the way I saw an actual patch of land. This is a far more significant sign of spring in upstate New York than the first robin.

But my initial glance of terra firma in 2003 brought only half-hearted joy. Which is exactly one half a heart more than George W. Bush possessed when he discarded reason, world opinion, and the growing awareness that if truth was the first casualty of war, we have already sustained massive losses, and commenced hostilities with what was called a decapitation strike on Baghdad on Tuesday, March 20, 2003. Leave it to the Pentagon to consider "decapitation" a sanitized term.

Once it started, the T v hacks seized upon each development as proof positive that Bush's decision to invade Iraq had been vindicated. It began during dawn coverage from the desert outside of Kuwait City on the first full day of the attack. After hours of a stationary night-vision shot from Baghdad and countless replays of the flashes and rumblings that U.S. bombs had caused earlier, networks needed something of visual interest for viewers. Here's what they came up with: *A dent in the desert allegedly caused by an Iraqi Scud missile.* As reporters at the scene of this supposed carnage reported through choppy satellite phone cam transmissions, anchors shook their heads and said things like,

"Woo that was close. You take care of yourself out there!" And, "This should silence all but the most irrational of Mr. Bush's critics." Yeah that *dented sand* really brought home the horror of war and certainly demonstrated the need for it.

One of the most consistently sickening elements of the month-long blitz of early G W I I coverage featured decommissioned brass holding court in little on-air war rooms while civilian anchors and reporters competed to see who could crawl the furthest up the retired officers' asses. At times C N N's Paula Zahn would have been completely off-camera had she not been wearing high heels.

I arrived in Boston to watch S U beat a scrappy Manhattan club in the opener and then come from behind to eliminate Oklahoma State in the second game. I went to both contests with my old comedy pal Don Gavin, who had played and coached a lot of basketball. We were right across from the Cowboy bench, and when their lead reached seventeen points, they were falling all over one another in fits of laughter reminiscent of the audience on *Def Comedy Jam*. I told Gav that I felt that this early celebration was a good sign for the Orange, and he betrayed where he just might have wagered a few dollars by replying, "I hope you're right, my son."

The basketball gods must have had Syracuse in their tourney bracke,t because by halftime the lead was shaved to six points, and by the middle of the second half the *Def Comedy* audience was looking for seats on the S U bench. Final score: Syracuse 68, Oklahoma State 56.

Bush's invasion also took an early lead that lulled its supporters into false confidence. His forces roared in and took Baghdad. But taking objectives is one thing. The trouble comes when those objectives must be held, when the target shooters become the targeted.

Bush has been sold to us by Karl Rove, a political low-blow champ who knows how to serve us shit and get us to pay extra for it by calling it *freedom filets*. After the conventional portion

of GWII was over and before it began to look too much like a
war of occupation with a steady increase in body counts of the
occupied and occupiers, Rove, the mother of all photo oppor-
tunists, decided to dress Junior in drag as a war hero and fly him
to address some troops. Finally we had found a Vietnam-era
MIA! The costumed court-appointed president landed on the
U.S. aircraft carrier *Abraham Lincoln* in a fighter jet as the ship
bobbed up and down in the hostile waters a mile or so west of
San Diego. Dubyahoo got up on the deck of the Honest Abe
and lied his ass off. He told us that his coalition had prevailed
and human rights had returned to Iraq. He told us that major
military operations were over. Unfortunately he forgot to tell the
Iraqi resistance, which had only just begun its major military
operations, which remain in high gear as I write this. The speech
is best remembered for two words written on a banner above the
court-appointed president. MISSION ACCOMPLISHED!

As I watched Bush make his jingoistic declarations, the Mission Accomplished banner made me think of two other words:
Oklahoma State.

He was just another cocky Cowboy riding for a fall.

In April 2004 I began work as a writer-commentator on Air
America Radio, the much-ballyhooed liberal AM talk start-
up. I was assigned to work with firebrand afternoon-drive host
Randi Rhodes, who is as tough as nails on the air and as fair
and decent and fun a person as I have ever worked with. And
man, does she know her stuff. Her listeners should get credit
hours. I arise early and comb the news for hypocrisy and other
outrages, so that as her day dawns, she has plenty of quips and
bullet points to choose from to add to whatever she has already
centered her sights upon.

The timing of the launch couldn't have been better. We took
to the air during the worst of months for the court-appointed
Bush administration. Former national security director Richard
Clarke's book *Against All Enemies* had just been released. It detailed

Bush's near-criminal disregard for repeated warnings leading up to 9/11. It also disclosed the Bush-Cheney determination to use the tragedy to needlessly foment war with Iraq.

The 9/11 commission hearings were making daily headlines, most of them extremely embarrassing for the Bush regime. It reached its nadir when Bush and Cheney testified together in private and not under oath. No record was kept of the meeting, but word did leak that whenever Cheney drank water, Bush gurgled.

This was also when Bob Woodward's book *Plan of Attack* caused an uproar because it documented that the only thing Bush and Cheney ever did was plan to attack, no matter how much lying, subterfuge, and shortsightedness their scheme required. The book hit the stores during the bloodiest month of the war, April 2004—a year after the littlest prez celebrated Halloween on May Day under the "Mission Accomplished" sign.

Iraq was becoming a full-fledged fiasco. The pot really boiled over in Fallujah, where four American contractors were killed and then literally torn limb from limb before their violated corpses were dragged through the streets. "Contractor" is often a euphemism for "mercenary" in this war. Sometimes it means a truck driver, but often it means dog-of-war. Hired killer. Dirty deeds done anything but dirt-cheap. I was sickened by what happened, because some things you wouldn't even wish on a dog of war. But I suspected that such overt and vicious acts weren't just a message; in all likelihood, they were a reply.

The siege of Fallujah followed and many $1,200-per-month U.S. service personnel died in a vain attempt to bring the killers of the thousand-dollar-a-day contractors to justice. Many, many more innocent Iraqi men, woman, and children also were killed, mostly by U.S. fire. After nearly a month of bloody standoff, the United States blinked and backed out, leaving a former general in Saddam's elite Republican Guard in charge. Then they decided that didn't look too good, and they found another Iraqi general, who after years of faithful service to Hussein apparently got into some trouble with his old boss. This was good enough for Bush, and the new old general was given the keys to the outskirts of the city, which was all the United States ever controlled. The people we went in to liberate were now left in the charge of the people we were supposedly there to drive from power. Worse, many of the soldiers who signed on with this general had been killing Americans just a week earlier.

During this mess Georgy Boy conducted a press conference that was more orchestrated than anything Aaron Copeland ever composed. He was stumped several times when asked if he ever made a mistake. He stammered, squirmed and allowed that he really couldn't come up with anything in such a pressure-packed circumstance as this slow-pitch softball tournament with the White House press corps. This from a man who had taken to swaggering around and calling himself our war president. While Bush was cracking under that intense strain, American soldiers had to summon the gumption to patrol the treacherous streets of Baghdad, hold tenuous positions on the outskirts of Fallujah and Najah, and suffer attacks in so many other hotspots in Iraq that the country had begun to resemble an octogenarian's birthday cake.

What brave words were they offered by their "war president"? A promise that he would be "resolute" and "stay the course." Which begged the question: exactly which goddamned course are you so resolutely staying, Mr., Bush? Because to the grunts on the ground in his hellish quagmire—who in many cases were being held beyond the one year of duty they had been told was their limit—the course was leading directly off a cliff. In April over 150 Americans died because George Bush sent them to an ill-planned, illegal war in Iraq. As May began, it looked like April's record might not stand for long.

One day the *New York Times* carried a picture on its cover that really brought it home to me. A grim-faced GI was shown

carrying a dead comrade in a body bag over his shoulder. That
poor kid will carry his buddy's corpse for the rest of his life.
Seeing the photo brought me back to the early 1970s and the
Syracuse Veteran's Administration Hospital. It was 1971, and
I was making daily visits to my father, in for an extended stay
when his vintage wwii post-traumatic stress disorder had
finally emotionally paralyzed him. Only after seeing that *Times*
picture did it strike me that Vietnam had to have aroused Phil
Crimmins' demons.

While spending time with Dad, I met the fresh casualties
of Vietnam. The Nam vets had obviously seen, been through,
and done so much that their terror and anguish permeated the
facility. Seeing that photo, I flashed back to riding in an eleva-
tor with a legless vet, a few years and a couple of centuries my
senior. I looked at him and tried to be friendly, and he just said,
"You don't want to know. You don't *fucking* want to know, man."
And he was right, but seeing him, I already knew more than
many people did at that point. I owe that guy and so many other
vets so much, because they made me into a peace activist. They
taught me that war was real and it blinded, maimed, and killed
people and that you'd better have an airtight reason for declaring
one, not just some chickenshit rhetoric about being resolute and
staying the course. George Bush never stayed anyone's course but
his own. He doesn't know what it means to have to man a check-
point at which you could either get blown up at any moment or
just as easily guess wrong and loose a burst of automatic weapon
fire into a car full of defenseless civilians. And then live with
it. Stay the course, indeed! The course is full of land mines, you
pompous blowhard.

The most expensive commodity required to fuel the war
machine—blood—is heavily infused with salt of the earth not
commonly found running through the veins of network execu-
tives, political spin doctors or court-appointed presidents. The
majority of casualties suffered by Bush's so-called coalition were

inflicted upon poor and middle-class kids. Kids who will live with this war long after the rest of us think it has ended. These kids will know the true horror of combat firsthand. Their families and friends will receive secondary exposure.

As many as 46 percent of the soldiers in this war are from poor rural areas like where I live in upstate New York. I couldn't count how many times I have driven by the bright yellow Army recruiting Humvee parked outside area high schools, waiting patiently as a recruiter was doing the bidding for the grim reaper's new motorized division.

Like Osama bin Laden, Saddam Hussein was just another little monster the United States helped bolt together. Two months after the Red, White, and Blue invaded Iraq the world knew that Hussein had been disarmed—*before* the invasion. The main premise for the war had been exploded . . . conventionally.

Few people, including those in the Middle East, lament the demise of Saddam Hussein, but to the Arab culture this war was not seen as an invasion of Saddam's Iraq—it was viewed as an attack upon the Islamic world. It won't soon be forgotten. These folks are still emotional over the Crusades. In Vietnam they have put America's assault upon their country behind them as best they could. Thirty years from now you won't find anyone in the Middle East burning incense for enemy souls lost in this war—embassies maybe, but no incense. Wars are easy to start but very difficult to end. They'll hold the Republican Convention in Paris before Gulf War II hatred for the United States even begins to subside in the Middle East. As the Bushists work toward the neo-con artist dream of Pox Americana, the Islamic fundamentalists will work just as hard to make sure that *a Jihad rain is gonna fall.*

Particularly now that we understand the message to which the killers of the contractors in Fallujah were responding. They were replying to, among other things, the word on the street of rape, torture, and murder in United States-run prison facilities.

Rape, torture, and murder that was directed at the notorious Abu Ghraib prison by private American *contractors* who worked for little-known but very profitable security firms: San Diego's Titan Corporation and Arlington, Virginia's, CACI International (Command and Control International is what it stands for, regardless of whether they admit it or not.)

Their sinister tasks were outsourced to break the chain of command. This provided plenty of plausible deniability for people like George Bush, Donald Rumsfeld, and Joint Chiefs of Staff Chairman General Ruchard Meyers. And just in case the chain of command issue did arise, all three of them could comfortably say they hadn't bothered to read a report that detailed these war crimes—even after it was two months old. They had more pressing concerns—mostly involving convoluting logic to continue to justify their insane war.

The other reason they had these thugs work the shadows for them was because Bush and his puppeteers had the foresight to pardon their operatives in advance for *any* crimes they may commit in Iraq. This was done with the May 2003 issuance of Executive Order 13303, which was designed primarily to place western oil companies above Iraqi law. It also allows so-called private security concerns to commit mayhem with caprice and no fear of justice. This is what happens in a society that has become too lenient with authority. After 9/11 America couldn't fall in line fast enough, and this played right into the authoritarian iron fists of the court-appointed Bush administration. Bush wasn't even in Washington at the will of the people, and now he had been given carte blanche to do as he saw fit. If that isn't a recipe for fascism, I need a new cookbook.

Executive Order 13303 was why American soldiers allowed the man who raped a fifteen-year-old Iraqi boy to walk out of the Abu Ghraib prison uncharged with any crime. They said they had no jurisdiction to charge him or any of the other private individuals who had, as Randi Rhodes so aptly put it, hung an

"Under New Management" sign over Saddam's torture chambers. Think of it, there the United States is, fighting its preemptive war, claiming the right to chase down evildoers anywhere, anytime, and any way it deems fit, but it lets boy-rapers slither away due to technicalities. The only law of the land in Iraq these days is the one George Bush signed that exempts these goons from any criminal liability. No wonder mercenaries sometimes end up getting drawn and quartered.

The Contractors-mercenaries are the Rosetta Stone of this entire mess. They lead us to Executive Order 13303, the rat hole Bush installed in Iraq as an easy escape route for his most nefarious operatives. They demonstrate with their brutal human-rights offenses Bush's true attitude toward the Iraqi people. And they make sense of something that has been bothering me for a few years. When the War on Terror was declared, I felt that its moral high ground had to be at least a tad compromised by all the Reagan-era death-squad diplomats who infested the court-appointed Bush administration. How could this rogues gallery run a war on terror? Was it a *it takes one to know one, hire Willie Sutton to case your own bank for you* deal? Maybe, but the presence of miscreants like John Negroponte, Richard Armitage, Otto Reich, Elliot Abrams, John Poindexter, Richard Perle, and so many more set my personal homeland security sensors on high alert.

With knowledge of Executive Order 13303 and how it overrides any other law, I now understand why these guys are back in action. Iraq is their dream situation. Bush has created a place where torturers and rapists and murderers can operate with impunity. They used to have to risk breaking American and international laws to fund and direct the savage killers they loosed upon Central America. Now all they have to do is nod and wink at an occasional bagman and the worst is done and the only people who suffer consequences are the victims of their extralegal activities.

Negroponte is about to be named as the super ambassador of the United States' super embassy in Baghdad. It's modeled after Wal-Mart. Its purpose is to destroy the competition and then it's *deal with us or go hungry*. All Hail the Uber Ambassador! The oil is the thing in Iraq, but there are billions of dollars being siphoned from other resources as well, like the U.S. Treasury. When people made the natural post–9/11 call for increased funding for intelligence and homeland security, they didn't realize how much of the increased resources would end up enriching the riff raff that run murky security outfits. Go to CICA's or Titan's websites, and their interests are made clear. Both list Homeland Security and the War on Terrorism as their top priority. When the rest of us saw horror on 9/11, these guys envisioned dollar signs. Homeland Security is the growth industry in war profiteering, and these guys have a basement office. Hundreds of millions of relatively unmonitored tax dollars are being given in no-bid contracts to outfits that, by presidential edict, needn't explain any of their activities in Iraq. And just in case you were wondering, both of these concerns operate offices and facilities all over America, AKA the homeland. Pleasant dreams.

At a time when the United States of America has issued a blank check to fight terrorism, do you suppose these global rent-a-cops are upset when their people go into Iraq and direct and participate in horrendous human rights offenses against Islamic people? The United States would have made fewer enemies had it blown up ten mosques full of women and children than it did when the photographs of the sexual, physical, and psychological abuse of prisoners at Abu Ghraib hit al Jazeera's airwaves. Do you think this scandal will serve to enrich or destroy Titan Industries or CICA? And do you think the people running these outfits don't know exactly what they are doing? These guys aren't stupid, they're just evil, and they play the game several moves ahead. They know they can survive whatever bad publicity they get for hiring civilian gangsters to run around Iraq in nylon jackets and overpriced sunglasses to commit atrocities that will inflame Islamic ire. And then all they have to do is sit back and smile while the political parties argue about who wants to put more money into the Department of Defense and Intelligence Communities to *combat this growing threat.*

Well, much of this threat is homegrown. Hamas and Arial Sharon provide perpetual mutual justification for the commission of continued atrocities in Israel and the occupied territories. Al Qaeda and the United States government are now expanding that same sort of futility to everywhere on Earth that is not under a polar icecap. And the greasy fingerprints of free agent provocateurs are all over everything.

If Americans really want to reduce terrorism, then we must regain control and responsibility for our own government and respond to injustice with justice. Domestically and internationally. To put it in terms even George W. Bush could fathom: you are either with justice or against it. 9/11 didn't give us a license to kill; it gave us a terrible new insight into why killing is wrong. It should have provoked us to make sure our own behavior exemplary. But the minute those towers went down, our unelected leader and his handlers set out to use the tragedy as justification for injustice after injustice.

The United States is wrong to covet the Iraqi oilfields. It's their oil, to do with as they see fit. It's our piggish consumption of that oil that we must control.

It's also their country to rebuild, and we must help by making sure the rebuilding processes revitalize Iraq and not the stock portfolios of a bunch of Texas fat cats.

America was wrong to preemptively attack a nation that had nothing to do with 9/11, did not have weapons of mass destruction, and was not a safe haven for Al Qaeda—and the rest of the world knows it.

We are wrong to continue to live in a society where a couple of guys growing a few marijuana plants can be deemed a crimi-

nal conspiracy and have all their assets seized while we allow
the likes of Titan and CICA and yes, Halliburton to conspire
to make this world exponentially more dangerous and therefore
more obscenely profitable for a few hyper-privileged corporate
criminals.

We are wrong to allow a phony little fraud like George W.
Bush speak in terms of his great faith when clearly all he believes
in is a god that has exempted him from the statutes that read:
"Thou Shalt Not Bear False Witness," "Thou Shalt Not Covet
Thy Neighbor's Property," "Thou Shalt Not Steal," and especially,
"Thou Shalt Not Kill."

George Bush's hubris has mass-produced the types of people
he hates worst—terrorists and Democrats.

By the time you read this I sincerely hope John Kerry has
become the president. At the moment he is standing aside and
letting Bush self-immolate but I expect him to pick up steam
this summer and eventually bring back the happy day when the
presidency is an elected office. In 2004 Christmas either comes
on Election Day or it doesn't come at all.

And by the way, when will we be spared further hogwash about how our military represents the best among us? It represents poor and middle-class kids. They certainly have the propensity to be the best among us. That said, the power elite have little or no respect for such people, save for when a microphone is on. Let's face it, the elite—the people who get to live like they are actually "the best among us"—don't let their kids anywhere near the military. If a diverse group of economically conscripted soldiers, attired in civilian garb, knocked on a rich person's door, they probably wouldn't be welcomed as if they were considered the cream of the American crop. More times than not, the police would be called. The cops wouldn't arrive looking to celebrate the heroism so obviously inherent in a bunch of kids who were raised in tough neighborhoods and educated in underfunded facilities. In fact, there is a decent chance that were one of the kids to do something dangerous—like reach for his identification—they'd all be chopped down like they were al Jazeera reporters.

twenty-four

War and Peace in a Ghost Town

"You always come out where you went in."

—Mark Twain

Anyplace, no matter how vital and lively to the naked eye, becomes a ghost town to those who have known it long enough. I'll go a bit further; if we survive for just an historical blink of the eye, we all become little ghost towns of our own. Individual relationships never really end, they just continue without interaction as our friends and relations predecease us. Favorite places become old haunts, often only recognizable when we look away and remember what once was.

Part One: The Ghost Town

Skaneateles is only a few hours away from where I now live, but I return to my hometown rarely these days because it isn't really *there* for me anymore. I don't know what's more painful, the hollowness of the business district (my friend Jimmy Huxford says, "It's not just Christmas tree shops anymore—now you can also buy anything your horse needs, except for food"), the ostentatious monstrosities that extremely wealthy people have hidden the lake behind, or the familiarity of the names etched in the stones of the village's two cemeteries.

I walk through Skaneateles, and not only are the stores I knew gone, but so are the merchants who were the closest thing to celebrities we had when I was growing up. Kindly Mr. and Mrs. Doyle at the old A & P, one of the last grocery stores that were long, narrow, tall, and anything but self-serve, were among the first to depart. Helpful Mr. Hahn at Hahn's Pharmacy, Mr. Talbot the soft touch for kids at Talbot's 5&10, and gruff Ed Riddler, the proprietor of Riddler's newsstand, have all vanished. I walk by the condos that are all that's left of the Colonial Theater and its owner Rube Cantor, who used to shut down the projector and threaten a movie house full of children in an attempt to bring us under some control at matinees that no sane adult ever attended twice. I can't pass the former Colonial without recalling the time I set off a smoke bomb on the ledge of the ticket-booth under the marquee, which was advertising the feature *Is Paris Burning?* I can still see it from the fifty strides I sprinted away before I turned to admire my prank. Perfect. A few steps down the street, and I'm remembering Dot and Joe McCauley, the parents of my friend Bill McCauley (1969 New York State heavyweight wrestling champ!) who are now as absent as the Western Auto they once owned and operated. Throughout my childhood I never had to swim at the park because I was always welcome at the lake rights behind McCauley's, maybe ninety seconds by bike down the hill from the home of Phil and Margaret Crimmins at 27 State Street. Now that I am older and pursue the grownup goal of keeping a home in as few pieces as possible by seeking goods and advice at chain hardware stores, I appreciate resourceful merchants like Earl Dando of Dando's Hardware and John Russell of Tucker Hardware, now long gone and replaced by a single corporate outlet that will never sell you one of anything that can be sheathed in plastic with five others.

The *Skaneateles Press's* familiar storefront is no more; the weekly is now relegated to the basement of the Milford Building, which I used to help Bill McCauley clean on nights and weekends. A chain called *Eagle Newspapers* owns it. It has a few pages of local interest pasted on the front of a cookie-cutter ad sheet that substitutes as the hometown paper for a dozen or so Central New York communities. Long gone is its former publisher, Wesley C.

Clark, dean of the Syracuse University School of journalism, a man with horrendously reactionary politics but a kindly manner toward a young sportswriter named Crimmins.

The ghosts loom above the village's street level as well. The affordable housing that once provided the apartments my boyhood pals Bob Brewer and John Considine were raised in have been replaced by pricey condos and high-end rentals. Even the field behind my house at the end of the municipal parking lot has been blacktopped to make more spaces for cars. No more ballgames in Crimmins stadium. They paved paradise . . .

Most of all I miss the dogs that ran free throughout the town until late in my youth. Their independence was the first canary to die in the mineshaft of our old ways. It used to be that everyone knew every dog in town. My boyhood companion was Lost, a black and tan (predominantly) German shepherd with floppy ears. He was named for the condition in which I discovered him—well, *one* of the conditions, anyway, there are too many Skinnys in Skaneateles. Lost roamed the town, and everyone and every other dog knew him. If he got in trouble, one of his many friends would either intercede or pick up the phone and dial 7322 (we didn't have cell phones, but four-digit dialing was pretty convenient), and I'd come sort him out. There aren't many doorways in downtown Skaneateles that weren't once occupied by good old Lost as he waited for me to finish a transaction. The smartest, most loyal hound I have ever known still roams free in the ghost town that I'm becoming.

Only the Skaneateles Bakery, now run by my friend Jim Coye, the son of its founder Dana Coye, and Roland's a great clothing store, particularly for working men, remain in a shopping area as impervious to working people as W's plans to heal the economy through further engorgement of the ultrawealthy. A few of the town's original taverns have withstood the test of time as well. The Sherwood Inn, where I was a dishwasher, groundskeeper, bar-back, and many other things at my first formal job, still does a great business, as does Morris' Grill, where my friends and I followed local custom by practicing our drinking on a nightly basis until we moved elsewhere or grew beyond the demographics of the crowd or simply learned the truth in Satchel Paige's maxim, *the social ramble ain't restful.*

I just received this news flash: the newsstand Riddler's is again Riddler's, but only for nostalgic reasons and only after someone bought it away from whoever named it Herb's for the past few decades. Of course it isn't in the original location of Riddler's, which used to be next to the old old post office until Ed lost his lease and had to move around the corner from Genesee street to Jordan Street. The old new post office (from the early 1960s) run by the late postmaster Paul Irving and home base to a staff of carriers to whom *neither snow nor sleet nor dark of night* was a much more challenging oath than the one their comrades almost anywhere else took, has now been relocated from right by the outlet directly across Genesee Street from Shotwell Park to Fennel Street, which is where most of the commercial expansion in the village now seems to transpire. This year the old new post office is being rebuilt into a hotel, the third to be added to the village in the last few years.

A new tract of fifty homes is materializing down Fennel Street at the site of Harvey's woods and the old sauerkraut factory, just the latest of the back lots, farmlands, and meadows that we romped in during my boyhood that have been sacrificed to what is inaccurately euphemized as progress. The oldest friend of all, Skaneateles Lake, teeters on the brink; its waters have been protected and kept reasonably pure by regulation, but it's only available to the wealthy except for the park, which has a swimming schedule that has been reduced to banker's hours for a scant ten or so weeks per year. Still you wonder how long it can hold up with the cigarette boats and jet skis noisily consuming the petroleum they don't spill directly in the lake as they describe their needless meanderings. And then there's all that wintertime salt from so many new parking lots running off to find its level in the lake below.

Most of what used to be sold on the streets of Skaneateles is now seven miles away at the Wal-Mart in Auburn—only the products are chintzier and their purchase provides almost no one with the decent lifestyles once enjoyed by the Talbots and Doyles and McCauleys. The other victims of this shift include domestic workers who used to manufacture goods for living wages, rather than the poor slave wage laborers of China, Guatemala, the Dominican Republic, and other distant locales whose toil fills the majority of purportedly All-American Wal-Mart's shelves. If it follows company policy, the Auburn Wal-Mart twice a day makes a wire transfer of money that used to feed the kids of the merchants of the main streets of Central New York. The loot goes to Arkansas; where only an extremely small percentage of the locals realize any benefit from it, unless they also wear the smock that announces that they, too work for a niggardly wage.

Skaneateles may think of itself as a special place, but the truth is it isn't special enough to avoid globalization, and as with the rest of the world, big money is wiping out the indigenous people. They can either fight and lose or collaborate and defeat themselves.

Part Two: Peace

Obviously I'm not the first person to return somewhere only to find it missing. Over the years Skaneateles and the surrounding region have gone through many changes. My sister, Mary Johanna Smith, who always seems to know about the most remarkable things, just told me an amazing story that she has been researching for several months. Skaneateles, a reactionary stronghold for the past century, used to be part of an upstate New York that was home to free thinkers and very progressive politics. It was the free thinkers of New York and New England who helped rescue Mark Twain from the backward notions with which he had been imbued as a lad in Missouri. Perhaps his Elmira in-laws caught a fellow named John Collins as he traveled through the area speaking at grove meetings with none other than Frederick Douglas in the early 1840s. Collins and Douglas toured at the behest of arch-abolitionist William Lloyd Garrison. I should have learned of it at Skaneateles Central School but never did. Garrison greatly admired Collins and wanted him to help show Douglas the ropes on the grove circuit. Douglas drifted from his traveling companion when Collins began to abandon the script to speak of issues that went beyond abolition.

At some point Collins must have spoken in Skaneateles, because by 1843 he had founded a commune about two miles north of the village. It was just one of many utopian communities organized by charismatic leaders in several upstate locations. Some maintained a strong religious element in their beliefs; Collins and his comrades did not—in general, anyway. As with most of the groups, the Collins commune was steeped in elements of Fourierism, a French philosophy based on the thoughts of Charles Fourier who was one of the original proponents of utopian socialism.

About 150 people joined the commune at its inception. Collins was a true believer in what was called moral suasion, a philosophy that truth and love could overcome any other power. The commune prospered, and as it grew, Collins and his comrades adopted formal articles of "belief, disbelief, and creed."

They were:

- Denial of revealed religion and the authority of the church and the Bible.

- Denial of the right of any government to use force to enforce its laws; hence members wouldn't vote, pay taxes, petition, serve on juries, do military duty or testify in courts.

- All goods were to be held in common—the right of individual property holding was denied.

- As marriage was assigned for happiness, the same should be dissolved when members had outlived their affection, and then new alliances could be made.

- The use of meat, narcotics and alcohol was prohibited. (Refraining from meat as a staple really helped the commune succeed fiscally.)*

John Collins refused to impose his will upon others. He believed in outlasting people with decency—carrying himself in such a moral fashion that others would see the sense in his behavior. When the commune began, Collins didn't speak out specifically against religion. When he did, it caused a rift between Collins and Quincy Johnson, a Syracuse lawyer and commune member who probably was a bit covetous of Collins' charismatic appeal. While a member of the community, Johnson maintained his religious beliefs on the side and freaked out when the commune began to sanction its own marriages. In addition to the pressure brought by Johnson, commune members had to deal more and more with relatives and others who could not tolerate their lifestyles. Commune members were harangued as the No Land-Free Lovers in the local paper, the *Skaneateles Columbian*.

The Commune countered with its own paper, *The Communitist*. Imagine, Communists in Skaneateles!

Despite all the outrage they provoked by assaulting the economic and sexual mores of the day, the commune was productive and a financial success. They had a farm, they sold crafts they manufactured, and they had their own school. Children were

---

* Source of points: The Skaneateles Communal Experiment 1843–1846 by L.G. Wells : a paper read before the Onondaga Historical Association February 13, 1953, Syracuse, New York.

instructed in astronomy, botany, art, geography, and philosophy. Members also contributed varying sums of money upon entering the cooperative endeavor. And it wasn't as if there was a constant orgy taking place on Jordan Road. Ostensibly all the commune believed was that if a marriage didn't work out, the parties should be free to seek happier unions. It wasn't as if property settlements presented much of a problem in a group that already pooled its resources.

Quincy Johnson ended up getting tossed out for undermining the commune—but not by Collins, who would never have taken such an overt action against anyone, lest he taint the morality of his suasion. Johnson kept up the assault from outside the three-hundred-acre commune, fueling local moral indignation concerning the commune's sexually liberated beliefs. The area of the commune was derisively labeled as No God.

The commune failed in an attempt to incorporate so as to alleviate outside pressures, but only after a long, divisive, and very public statewide struggle. Much like modern peace activists, the commune member's activities were pathologized by their contemporaries. *Imagine people agreeing with a French philosophy of nonviolence!* By 1846 Collins, having decided that mankind wasn't yet creative enough for socialism, threw in the trowel and left the commune. It collapsed without him. He left all he'd invested in the commune and went to California, where he became involved in mining and land auctions before evaporating into the ether of the ages. As his former fellow commune members tried to reenter local society, their castigation was so intense that they fearfully destroyed most of the records that documented their brief way of life. If they were to decide to make a tourist attraction at the site of the former Skaneateles Commune, it would have an inventory as shallow as that of the post-preemptive strike Iraq National Museum. Of course it will be a few more eons before Skaneateles realizes that there is nothing embarrassing about having been home to a nonviolent vegetarian commune that questioned the repressive sexual standards of a backward era.

Part Three: War

Only a mile or so back toward the village from the site of the old commune stands the Robert J. Hydon American Legion Post 237. Hydon was the first Skaneateles resident to die in World War I, not in gallant battle but on a Navy ship in the great influenza outbreak of 1918. The large semicircular approach to the facility is named after a genuine Grade A American war hero, General Jonathan "Skinny" Wainwright, a native of Walla-Walla, Washington, but a son-in-law of Skaneateles.

Wainwright was a thin man long before Douglas MacArthur left him in command of Allied forces in the Philippines when Dugout Dug made the departure from the island nation so necessary for his overhyped return. Wainwright was known as the last of the fighting generals for his propensity for joining the troops on the front lines during combat. His wife, Adelle Holley Wainwright, departed the Philippines and sat out the war with her mother in Skaneateles. Her husband led a courageous but hopeless effort on the small rock fortress island of Corregidor until May 6, 1942. His troops were all but out of ammunition and other supplies and being subjected to a massive Japanese aerial assault. Finally he wrote President Roosevelt: "There is a limit of human endurance and that limit has long since been passed. Without prospect of relief, I feel it is my duty to my Country, and to my gallant troops, to end this useless effusion of blood and human sacrifice. With profound regret and continued pride in my gallant troops, I go to meet the Japanese commander."

Many mistakenly believe the troops that surrendered at Corregidor were then subjected to the infamous Bataan Death March, but this didn't happen. The death march was over twelve days before Corregidor fell. Instead they were ferried across the bay to Manila, where they were forced to march in ignominious review. Wainwright was made to parade past his own defeated ranks, who managed to show their respect for him by a rising their starved, sickly, and wounded bodies to attention as he passed.

In late July 1942 General George C. Marshall suggested that Wainwright be awarded a Medal of Honor. MacArthur, unforgiving of Wainwright for not dying before surrender, protested and quashed the idea saying, among other things that "It would be a grave mistake which later on might well lead to embarrassing repercussions to make this award."

Wainwright spent over three years in Japanese prisoner-of-war camps, where he was tortured and starved, but his greatest agony was the guilt he felt over having surrendered. No one who knew Wainwright believed he'd have ever given up if only his own life was on the line; no, he only relinquished his command to save the lives of thousands who faced sure slaughter. His days in Japanese confinement were spent without any knowledge of the medal he nearly received in absentia. In fact, Skinny spent his captivity convinced that he would face humiliation for the surrender if he survived the ordeal. The highest-ranking American POW was liberated by Russian troops at a Manchurian camp in late August 1945. Days later he was on the deck of the USS *Missouri* for the Japanese surrender. A suddenly magnanimous MacArthur made sure that Wainwright was front and center at that ceremony and even gave the extremely malnourished general the first pen he used to countersign the document.

Skinny then returned home to a hero's welcome. On September 19, 1942, the last fighting general, Jonathan Wainwright, and his bride Adelle were guests of honor at the White House, where, during a meeting with Harry Truman, the president asked Wainwright to step outside to the Rose Garden to "continue their conversation." It was there that a flabbergasted Wainwright was surprised with the Congressional Medal of Honor for his heroic wartime service. This time MacArthur knew enough to keep his mouth shut.

The commendation read: "[Wainwright] Distinguished himself by intrepid and determined leadership against greatly superior enemy forces. At the repeated risk of life above and beyond the call of duty in his position, he frequented the firing line of his troops where his presence provided the example and incentive that helped make the gallant efforts of these men possible. The final stand on beleaguered Corregidor, for which he was in an important measure personally responsible, commanded the admiration of the Nation's allies. It reflected the high morale of American arms in the face of overwhelming odds. His courage and resolution were a vitally needed inspiration to the then sorely pressed freedom-loving peoples of the world."

The next big event was in Skaneateles, where on September 24, 1945, Wainwright was the guest of honor in the biggest parade the village has ever known. New York State Supreme Court Judge Charles Major sounded like the young boy he was at the time when he remembered, "the parade was so long that it went all the way up the hill on East Genesee Street, turned around and . . . there were columns marching on both sides of the street."

Thirty-five marching bands helped contribute to the record-setting parade, which also included United States Secretary of War Robert Porter Patterson.

"I saw it on Movietone News, down at Camp Lejeune," recalls Dave Huxford (Jimmy's father), of another moment when Skaneateles had arrived on the proverbial map. The General had turned sixty-two years old just nine days before his appearance on the deck of the Missouri. Gaunt and sallow, he looked ninety. Ever the soldier, he managed to stand at firm attention during the historic proceedings, just as his beleaguered troops had managed to get to their own feet in Manila out of respect for a man who spent a lot more time at the front with them than

Douglas MacArthur ever did. And when Wainwright showed up, it wasn't with a film crew.

Wainwright didn't stay in Skaneateles long after the parade. His white horse however remained a fixture in the town. Another veteran, Bob Hoffman, rode it in every parade until the horse died many years later. Much like Bill Clinton during his visit in 1999, Wainwright's every move was watched and overreacted to by excited townsfolk. This is bad enough for a president, with a full staff and serious security, but must have been hell for a man who a month earlier had been rotting away in a Japanese prison camp, eating his heart out over a decision that only others with the perspective of time and distance could see was unavoidable and, in its own way, quite heroic. They hadn't found a name for post-traumatic stress disorder back when General Wainwright rode through Skaneateles waving at the massive crowds on the parade route. Had the malady been identified, perhaps people would have realized that the last thing he needed was to have thirty-five marching bands announce his presence.

By all reports Wainwright got out of town soon after the hoopla and found his way to San Antonio, Texas, where he lived with Adelle until his death at the age of seventy in September 1953. He was buried in Arlington National Cemetery between his father, a cavalry officer killed in the shameful U.S. war against the Philippine people at the turn of the century, and Adelle, who died in 1970.

Just about when Wainwright was being feted in Skaneateles and Washington, a future commander of the Robert J Hydon Post #237 of the American Legion, naval Gunnery Control Officer Philip Crimmins was on shore patrol in the vanquished nation of Japan. My father had been not far from fallen Corregidor when he participated in the largest naval engagement in the history of warfare, the Battle of Leyte Gulf. Had Japanese intelligence not intercepted a plea to Admiral Bull Halsey from the U.S. fleet engaged in the watery conflagration, they wouldn't have broken away from the conflict, and Dad probably never would have lived to receive the Bronze Star with a V for valor that he was awarded for bravely leading the charge to extinguish a fire that was about to spread to the fuel dump of the destroyer from which he fought his portion of the war. As a gunnery control officer my father always had binoculars at the ready, and so at Leyte he watched helplessly as a ship carrying one of his best friends was hit and went down. His friend didn't make it. Throughout the battle, with his enhanced view, Dad witnessed sailors from both sides fight desperately for their lives in shark-infested waters that were literally on fire with the burning fuel that had spilled from stricken vessels. The horror didn't end with the war. He told me of seeing an American minesweeper strike a cluster of the devices it was meant to clear from Tokyo Harbor. Although he had seen many men die during the war, watching that vessel's crew go down after the hostilities had supposedly ended was something my father could never reconcile.

One night he told me that the biggest regret of his entire military service happened when he was on shore patrol in Japan. An elderly Japanese man was traversing a long bridge that crossed over a railroad yard fifty or so feet below. Coming in the other direction was a large U.S. marine. My father had already passed and nodded to the old man, who had asked him for a cigarette. Phil was an athlete whose football career had been delayed by his years at war, but he planned to and did return to play college ball (at Catholic University in DC). He never picked up the smoking habit because even during the golden age of tobacco, he'd heard that smoking was bad for one's wind. Dad deferentially gestured that he was sorry that he had no cigarettes and proceeded across the bridge. A few more paces down the walkway he heard the Japanese man try to bum a smoke off the marine. Dad glanced back to see the marine pick up the beggar with both hands, raise him over his head, and toss the poor fellow to his death below. My father stood in shock as the marine bustled by, mumbling profanely about any Japanese person with the nerve to ask him for anything. When my father gathered himself, he ran down to aid the victim but it was too late, he had died on impact. My father never forgave himself for not arresting that marine. "That was my job, and not just because I was on shore patrol. I saw a murder and did nothing about it."

True enough, but he saw that murder after he had spent the last few years living with death and carnage. I don't have to estimate whether my father had post-traumatic stress disorder because I know that he did, and I know that's what froze him. My father was a good and brave man who, like most of us, would rather risk his life to save others than to ever take life from someone. But he had directed guns during the war that helped kill many, and he knew it. And he was wracked with survivor guilt for all the guys who didn't come away alive from Leyte Gulf, Tokyo Harbor, and even a Japanese railroad yard.

After the bridge incident my father ended up in, of all places, Hiroshima. Ever a soft touch, Dad was immediately smitten with the kids who had survived the world's first nuclear bombing. Unable to do much for them, he began using all of his sugar rations on Hershey bars, which he distributed to the kids, many of whom were orphans. He also played baseball with them in the rubble of the city. A few other softhearted gobs saw what Dad was up to, and soon his kindness became an enterprise of a few really good men. They began trading their alcohol ration cards (or however they doled it out) for the sugar allotments of other sailors. It was all turned into candy. Word of this operations spread quickly among the children, and soon they had to take measures to create an equitable distribution of the chocolate. When the ration cards came out, Dad and his buddies pooled their resources and loaded up on candy. They would then allot a certain amount for each day until the next ration cards were distributed. Every afternoon Phil Crimmins and his pals would meet the kids, count how many were there, and then take and break the Hershey bars into the little squares they came in. Then they divided the number of kids into the number of squares and determined how much chocolate each kid got each day. That's right, my father the old right-winger was a Hershey bar socialist! After the war his deterioration continued when he married and moved to a known *communitist* community.

Eventually Dad and his pals were about to be shipped out of Hiroshima, and so he bought another load of chocolate and entrusted a few of the older kids to employ his distribution policy. He called it the honor system, but I like to think of it as *moral suasion*. At their final meeting the kids, who spoke virtually no English, insisted that my father follow them down to, of all places, a railroad yard. There, between the width of the track, on a small patch of land that had not been flash-fried by the bomb because it had been shadowed by a railroad engine, was a pitiful little garden. From it the children pulled a few meager baby carrots and proudly presented them to my father. Perhaps they figured he needed to get something other than refined sugar in his diet. Most likely they wanted to give two gifts to the man, who in his own nutritionally illiterate manner, had found a way for a few American sailors to give them their all. The first and obvious gift was the carrots. The second and subtle gift was the knowledge that in a few weeks the crops would grow and they would be able to feed themselves. I never found out if my father ate those carrots. That would answer a lot of questions.

Last year the unelected son of another World War II vet landed on the deck of the aircraft carrier *Abraham Lincoln* to tell us lies about how his war on Iraq was over. Perhaps if he had actually flown in a fighter jet in combat during the Vietnam War instead of spending all his time avoiding so many National Guard roll calls in Texas, he would have known that wars never really end. His handlers bragged that the martial footage of Bush's appearance on the *Lincoln* would make great campaign film. They were right; John Kerry would be crazy not to use it.

My father's war continued in nightmares that provoked screams that shattered the evening peace of my mother and her children. Of course compared to families in Baghdad and so many other places, our plight was minor. We only lived with distant repercussions of war. Our sleep was only disturbed by memories of explosions, not the real thing. Growing up I thought that everyone had pictures of their father standing in front of the pretzeled girders of wreckage from a nuclear blast.

Dad could be difficult, to say the least, but he was also a sweetheart who would drop everything to assist anyone in need. To make sense of the horror he had survived, he decided that so long as something was wrapped in the American flag, it was OK. He was funny and smart and a good guy's good guy, but most people headed the other way if they had any inkling he was about to start talking politics.

In the summer of 1972 my mother, who had lived with a very difficult man for twenty-three years, finally gave up and separated from him. My father had a habit of returning from business trips just long enough to change his clothes and head somewhere important like Syracuse football practice, leaving my mother holding the bag that contained me, my sisters, and a home that was built in 1824 and often in need of upkeep and repairs. How she lasted as long as she did, I'll never know.

Next my father lost his job (as a school-furniture salesman) of twenty-two years. At that point he went into a deep depression and lay on the couch in a near-catatonic state for weeks. With the help of our friend good friend Ralph Cheche, I got him admitted to the VA hospital in Syracuse. It was at that Veterans' hospital that I first met a lot of Vietnam vets, and they told me a much different story about the war from the one I had read about or heard anywhere else. I asked several of them if I should join up and do my bit, and they either laughed at me or severely chastised me for even considering something that stupid. The next year I got my draft number, 109. They took people to within a few numbers of mine, but they never got to me and I never had to make the agonizing decision so many other male Baby Boomers confronted.

For the rest of his life my father was in and out of veteran's facilities. In my opinion, rather than give him the proper psychotherapy he needed for his untreated spiritual war wounds, they just turned this American hero into a guinea pig for big pharmaceutical concerns. Along the way he developed a palsied neurological disorder that was never explained. Doctors told Mary Jo that an MRI he had had ten or so years before he died showed abnormalities in his brain that they had never before encountered. Years earlier a VA doctor had assured me that my father's palsy had nothing to do with his nuclear veteran status. Yeah, sure, and the weather in Skaneateles has nothing to do with my sarcasm, either.

That my father's brain was uncharted territory comes as no surprise to Mary Jo, my other sister, Virginia Westcott, or me but we all knew that whatever had happened to it, his capacity to love us was never even slightly compromised. After entering the hospital in 1972, my father was rarely ever close to being himself again. MJ made constant trips to Syracuse to help him keep his affairs in order and to engage in gallant battle with the VA on his behalf. When he could travel, Ginny always welcomed him at her home in Virginia, where he enjoyed the company of grandchildren and dogs. Busy with my stupid comedy career, I never saw him as often as I should have, but Dad was great about it. Most young people who go into comedy face the prospect of freaking out their parents. When I told Dad, he said, "Great! I always wanted to be a comedian." He could have been a fabulous comic, but war got in the way.

Until I learned more about my father and all he had been through, I had a very difficult time sorting out my rather complex relationship with the man. But to learn of his war experiences and how he ended the endeavor feeding and playing with chil-

dren on the radioactive streets of Hiroshima was to discover a
context that allowed me to find a peace that had eluded him. My
father was like so many other people: he often exhibited bizarre
and even irrational behavior, but if you could find the map to his
ghost town, he made considerable sense. Put simply, the more we
look to find context for others, the less we will be able to simply
write those people off. The same can be said of races, religions,
genders, sexual persuasions, and even nations. Put more simply,
there is sanity at the source. And peace is sanity.

On July 16, 1994, at the Syracuse, New York, Veterans' Hospital, World War II finally ended for my father. He is now one
of those names carved in stone just to the right of the entrance
of St. Mary's of the Lake Catholic Cemetery, right across from
Wainwright Drive and just down the street from Skaneateles's
only socialist ghost commune. Each year when winter ends, I
travel to Skaneateles and tidy up my father's gravesite. Then
I stroll through the cemetery and visit with other friends. As I
walk along, I think of war and of all the people who will never
again breath fresh spring air because of it. And then I will quit
my melancholy lollygagging, go home and get on with the
crucial work of stopping the next war before it has a chance to
never end.

Don't get me wrong; I'm not calling this Vietnam. In Vietnam they have put America's assault on their country behind them. Thirty years from now you won't find anyone in the Middle East burning incense for all the souls lost in this war—embassies maybe, but no incense.

They'll hold the Republican Convention in Paris before Gulf War II hatred for the United States even begins to subside in the Middle East.

A Jihad rain is gonna fall.

twenty-five

The Repression Will Be Televised
(Try Radio for Revolution)

*B**y the time you read this I will have joined my old friends Lizz Winstead, Janeane Garofalo and Sam Seder, plus several new ones, including Randi Rhodes and Al Franken on the Air America Radio Network. I love radio because it allows you to do more than imply inflection. Below is a piece I did on a Christmas Coup Comedy Players show on Pacifica radio's New York affiliate WBAI on January 1, 2004. Since it was a holiday, the Bushists had the terror strobe light turned up to "disco." My comments were fraught with inflection; use your imagination and add your own. After that, tune us in and you won't have to guess where the emphasis belongs.*

Happy New Year to everyone out there in the land of the good old Orange, White, and Blue! And special warm wishes go out to all the revelers who, as extras, played starring roles in last night's Times Square celebration in New York City. In the waning seconds of 2003, you passed through more safety checkpoints than a high-end Volvo, only to be scanned and screened again and again by electronic probes—*I'm Proud to Be an American, Please Squat Over the Device*—just so you could wear wacky glasses that utilized the double zero that is at the heart of any court-appointed Bush administration year. Yes, here's to all hardy New Yorkers who, at the direction of automatic weapon-wielding cops, were forced into a *sardinically* brutal crush of alcohol- and drug-free people at a celebration where the only buzz came from a gigantic sound system that blared music with messages so diverse and innovative that it was hard to tell if the songs had been written by Toby Keith or Lee Greenwood.

I'm Proud to Be an American, Please Squat Over the Device!

Yes, The only high that was welcome in Times Square last night was of the steroidal variety, because let's face it, the N Y P D has a bigger muscle-juice problem than the National Football League, Vince McMahon's pro wrestling confederation, and Barry Bonds' press agent, combined. *If you won't submit to further scrutiny, I'll just have to get down off this horse and forcibly make you comply with the patriotic catch phrase that will sweep the nation in 2004: I'm Proud to Be an American, Please Squat Over the Device!*

Ah yes, it was an unforgettable night in New York, the city so nice they named it twice . . . before strip-searching everyone four times.

I'm Proud to Be an American, Please Squat Over the Device!

I watched the proceedings on Dick Clark's Rocking New Years Eve because in a country where a court-appointed president can be considered a symbol of democracy, why shouldn't cryogenically extended Clark be synonymous with rock and roll—especially now that he has added Fatherland Security Chief Tom Rigid—A K A Clutch Cargo—as his permanent cohost?

Rigid was great as he provided color-coded commentary on how the terrorists would never win so long as we remained PROUD TO BE AMERICANS, PLEASE SQUAT OVER THE DEVICE!

And who among us didn't feel at last a symbolic kick in the ball as the orb descended in the ultimate instants of 2003, flashing every color in Rigid's authoritarian rainbow before finally hitting bottom and igniting the words that inspire all truly patriotic Americans: WE'RE PROUD TO BE AMERICANS, PLEASE SQUAT OVER THE DEVICE!

Who among us didn't stifle a tear of nostalgia as that most important annual message of all illuminated the midnight Times Square gathering? It said but two words—Discover Card—but they are two words powerful enough to sober millions of Americans each January. And although they may read as Visa or Massacard to many of us, those two modest words; Discover Card, reminded us that even though Christmas is for kids, the rest of the year belongs to loan sharks. Discover Card, the domestic answer to the IMF. The letters on that sign were formed in plastic and ignited by an energy industry for which we have sent our children to assault a sovereign state under false pretenses, making the year we just departed sure to join other needless war years in the litany of questionable American military incursions.

Happy 2004! WE'RE PROUD TO BE AMERICANS, PLEASE SQUAT OVER THE DEVICE!

Yes, discover another year of inordinate debt exponentially compounded by holiday spending sprees through which we attempt to patch the ever-expanding void in our national soul by filling it with material goods, manufactured by laborers who work unpaid overtime in foreign sweatshops straight through Hanukah, Christmas, Kwanza, and New Years, not to mention Thanksgiving, Saint Valentines Day, May Day, and especially Flag Day, when the demand for the totemic salutes to our American Freedom, a commodity so precious to us that we will soon build a 1776 foot tower in its memory at the site of the World Trade Center. The WTC, where the court-appointed Bush administration made sure that its first act in response to the terrorist inferno was to feed it with every copy of the Bill of Rights it could lay its hands upon.

Happy 2004! WE'RE PROUD TO BE AMERICANS, PLEASE SQUAT OVER THE DEVICE!

It is your duty as Americans to Have a Happy New Year until you are advised otherwise by the court-appointed Bush administration that reminds us: Repression is the better part of valor.

Now once more—all together: WE'RE PROUD TO BE AMERICANS, PLEASE SQUAT OVER THE DEVICE!

So come on, America, let's welcome the infant 2004 by rising together and saying in one voice—WE'RE PROUD TO BE
AMERICANS, PLEASE SQUAT OVER THE DEVICE! Don't
you feel like a better person already? Get out of your seats and
scream louder than a right-wing talk show when confronted by
logic: WE'RE PROUD TO BE AMERICANS, PLEASE SQUAT
OVER THE DEVICE!

WE'RE PROUD TO BE AMERICANS, PLEASE SQUAT
OVER THE DEVICE!

Postscript

Dear John,

I'm sorry, but there's no other way to put this: I can't see you anymore—at fundraisers that is. If Whoopi Goldberg's comments about court-appointed President Bush at your recent New York show-biz gala were enough to stir up a media storm, the Weather Channel would need to break out its full hurricane crew to cover any joint appearance you and I might make.

From what I understand, Whoopi used a "bush" *double* entendre to insult your opponent. If you caught my act lately, you'd have a hard time finding anything but a *single* intention in my shows. I am urging my fellow Americans to do whatever it takes to drive this government Of the Cronies, By the Cronies, and For the Cronies from stolen office. If pitchforks and torches are necessary, I stand ready to authorize their use.

I was sick of these people before they stepped off the reviewing platform on January 20, 2001. This was back when they came to town promising to "return ethics to Washington." (Keep your enemies closer, I suppose.) Three and a half years later, the entire nation is colicky—nauseated by the policies and conduct of a regime that, to put it in the parlance of old-school Boston political insults, is so crooked it could hide behind a corkscrew.

And so you are our hope. Our only hope. Some of my old political allies are vexed with me for placing hope in you. The main reason they question me is that you signed off on letting

an administration rife with self-proclaimed Christians cast the
first stone in Iraq.

Oh, sure, you have plausible reasons for having done so. Anyone with a whit of political savvy knew Saddam was a bad guy
long before Donald Rumsfeld began appearing with him on
Kodachrome in the 1980s. And the pre-war human-rights situation in Iraq was undeniably deplorable. But the alibi for falling
in line that goes something like, "Well, the administration has
produced compelling intelligence information" never clicked
with anyone who has even a passing familiarity with the cia's
odious track record. And giving this administration the benefit
of the doubt certainly does not demonstrate the grasp of reality
that we should expect from a leader.

I understand the political pressure you felt, but still, you're a
brilliant guy and had to know what a load of hooey was being
dumped on us. I further estimate that the hard-bitten among
your insiders advised, "Look, you know we can always just say
they lied to us," and considering who was trumping up this war,
that was a pretty safe fall-back position. But please, you did a
nice job investigating and exposing much of this crew back when
terrorism was a central component of Saint Ronald Reagan's not-
so-secret foreign policy. And so when the same gang of thugs who
help facilitate death-squads in Central America came forward
as the defenders of innocence and champions of democracy, you
should have marched right outside of the Capitol and joined the
hundreds of thousands of us who were in the streets screaming,
"Noooooo! Don't do it!"

Well, Senator, we told you so.

Some of my lefty pals won't forgive you and I can see their
point. Nevertheless, I refuse to join their circular firing squad. I
know how to face political reality myself, and if ever there were
an occasion for compromise, this is it. I don't value my moral
purity more than the lives of countless innocents. My stridence
withers when I consider how much suffering would result if the

Bush regime extends beyond next January. Someday, George W. Bush's administration will be labeled for what it brought us to: the "New Low." Under your leadership, even a slight trajectory of improvements in health-care, environmental regulation, civil liberties, and workers' rights will have to be measured against the all-too-imaginable speed at which of these vital matters would reach even newer lows during a second Bush term. So I won't be doing any benefits for Ralph Nader this year, no matter how much the Heritage Foundation offers.

In this system, at this time, we have but two options; one is George W. Bush and Dick Cheney. The other is you and John Edwards. To say there is no difference between the pairs of you would be to articulate political naïveté of the worst sort. No matter what you do as president, the next four years will be better than they would be if we Elect Bush, Just This Once. Because I know you will begin to undo some of the New Low damage that's been inflicted on us. If you win, no one with even shadowy ties to the Ku Klux Klan will be appointed to the federal bench. I doubt that you'll ever bring in lobbyists from the chemical industry to write environmental law. I'm relatively certain that you won't allow national parks to be used for monster-truck rallies.

Even though you're a hunter (at least, according to your Red State campaign ads), you won't be persuaded that your fellow outdoor-carnage enthusiasts need automatic weapons because deer attack in waves. I believe that even though you are a Christian, you'll never take it to the cultish lengths that our current crackpot-in-chief does—which is to say you are not among the lunatics who think that if we can provoke one final fatal conflict between Islam and Judaism, it will end the world and begin a members-only rapture.

And I know that if you're elected, you'll be the most powerful person in the world . . . and you'll do a better job of it than Dick Cheney has. I like the Edwards-Cheney match-up; it says you understand that trial lawyers play a huge role in the battle to keep this country safe and just. It gives us a choice between a ticket that includes a trial lawyer and one that doesn't believe in trials. For that matter, it hasn't much use for laws either. But the most important part of this November's choice is the one between you and George W. Bush. Your charisma has suffered a very unfair assault. I realize that to keep your "all things to all people" advisers happy, you must make overly qualified, platitude-heavy statements of little substance. When I hear you preface anything with "I believe," I know I have time to wash, dry, iron, and fold a load of laundry before you get to telling us exactly what it is you hold dear. But hey, that's politics. In any case, if this race is decided on charisma, then you're Clark Gable and John F. Kennedy rolled into one compared to the beady-eyed placeholder who now occupies the Oval Office. A president is supposed to instill confidence. This guy's press conferences are so heavily scripted that I am always disappointed when Roger Ebert fails to give them a thumbs-down. If charisma is an issue in this campaign, it has to disadvantage the man who tortures the language as if it were a detainee at the Abla Gaduu uh, err, Abo Galabaaga, oh never mind.

No matter how anyone tries to spin it, the American people are sick of Bush. The wise among us appreciate that his leadership has brought us to the sorry point where it's become our patriotic duty as Americans to be ashamed of our nation. The rest are ready to do him in because, as Americans with God-given short attention spans, they've had enough of a guy who keeps whining about "freedom-haters." They are ready to reach for the remote and click over to anything but George W. Bush.

Some pundits maintain that Bush is more likable than you, yet all but the pathologically deluded know otherwise. Although you seem like a refined and somewhat inaccessible Ivy Leaguer, it's obvious that you got into Yale because you are a smart person. Everyone knows that somewhere there is a guy with a degree from Brown because George W. Bush legacyed him out of four years in New Haven. Bush is the kind of rich boy who would get even with you for beating him out for the baseball team by having his father get your father fired as the greenskeeper at the country club. Americans have the innate ability to sniff out that kind of stench on a man, which is why we didn't elect this latter-day Sonny Drysdale in the first place.

I am endorsing you and voting for you, Senator, because you have done two things a simpering daddy's boy like George W. Bush never would: you have marched both to and against war. As a result, I have great hope that when your decisions result in life or death, they will not be reached via the swerving, dangerous, and ridiculous path of a drunken frat boy.

I must compliment whoever on your staff came up with the ingenious idea to leak word that you didn't want to release your military records. Man, did the rubes from Texas ever fall for that slick hunk of Yankee bait, or what? Once you released the documents, the only imaginable reason for your reticence was humility. Not only did you show up Bush with your stellar record, you reminded the country that military records can in fact be produced.

It's great that the Democratic National Convention is being held in Boston. Despite all the worst efforts of the court-appointed Bush administration, the Hub is still a bastion of free speech—providing, that is, you don't mind walking your picket sign into town on I-93. I trust you will make some grand and broad gesture to reach out to the protesters to make it clear that you understand that dissent is the lifeblood of democracy.

There would be far fewer protesters if not for the all-consuming issue of the Iraqi quagmire. My view can be articulated in just three words: more is worse. But as you may recall, I have never been a man of few words, so let me add: to continue to waste American, "Coalition," and Iraqi lives and resources in this illegal, horribly planned, and cynical effort to restore a nation that is nothing more than a failed eighty-four-year-old British construct would be a blunder of historic proportion. This war is a failure. The Iraqi people hate America because Americans, attacking from the self-proclaimed moral high ground, have brought violence and degradation to their homelands. The only ones to benefit from not getting out as soon as possible have been the war profiteers and terrorist recruiters. Maintaining Western hegemony over Iraqi oil is not worth the human price that will be exacted so long as one survivor of this conflict lives with its memory.

And I know you know about war memories, John. I know you still live with the horror you saw in Vietnam. To your everlasting credit, you continued your heroic behavior upon returning from duty. Were it not for hero vets like you, the draft would have surely taken me in the early '70s. And I'd have gone because I was a rural boy who didn't know any better—so I owe you and the entire anti-war movement for my life. Had I fought, I might have survived physically but I wouldn't have escaped becoming one of the emotional fatalities. We will have tens of thousands of such cases returning from Iraq (and Afghanistan)—that is, if Bush ever stops exiling them with extended tours of duty.

You understand that the saddest thing that can be said about our nation today is that it would rather create veterans than care for them. In the coming years, we need a president who will guarantee that the vets of our current wars come home to compassionate, top-notch care and support. I can think of no one who would be more dedicated to carrying out that policy than you, Lieutenant Kerry.

There will be plenty of your fellow vets at DNC protests. I know you can never view them as enemies. I also know that at least part of your reluctance to directly advocate an Iraqi pullout is that it could be seen by the troops in the field as undermining their already treacherous circumstances. But I am taking you at your word that you will use the power of the presidency to conscript the rest of the world into bringing peace, order, and justice to Iraq. Perhaps your boldest words have been to suggest that Arab nations be brought into the process. Now there's an idea.

So here's the deal, John. We get you in, and you get us out. A little of the old in-and-out never hurt anyone. I guess I do stoop to double entendres on occasion—just another reason to avoid me for the next three months. You'll do fine without me. If you need me to perform during the inaugural weekend, I'll be happy to reassess my position.

With best wishes for great success,

BARRY CRIMMINS

Acknowledgments

With special thanks to Karen Crist, Lloyd the Dog, my mother Margaret Hooe, Kevin Bochyncski, all the comics, journalists, activists, and friends. And special thanks to the boys from Skaneateles and the editorial staff of the Boston Phoenix, particularly, my longtime editor Clif Garboden, and to the great Randi Rhodes and everyone at Air America. Thanks also to Lars Reilly and Dan Simon for their remarkable help on this project. This book is full of my friends and the world is full of the rest of them.

And of course, my father, Philip Owen Crimmins.

About the Author

Barry Crimmins grew up in Skaneateles (an Indian name meaning "small lake surrounded by fascists"), New York. In his time he has worked with many comedy greats, near-greats, and ingrates, and his exploits have included a stint writing for Dennis Miller. Crimmins currently writes for Air America Radio and lives in Troupsburg, New York.